PowerPoint Slides That Work!

Show + Tell for Grownups

●●●●

Steven B. Levy

A DayPack Book

4 6 8 9 7 5 3

DayPack Books   ●   Seattle, WA

For Anya, Miriam, and Jeremy: Thank you. Again.

Thanks also to Bill Speros, Christian Fuenfhausen, John Rapp, Kelly Ray, and Marc Lauritsen for suggestions along the way.

Contents

INTRODUCTION

This book cannot solve all of your presentation problems. If you mumble, it will not serve as a microphone. If you don't know your subject, it will not boost your expertise. If you're running late, it will not be your time machine.

But if your slides are unappealing, if they're boring, and most importantly, if the material on screen works against rather than supports what you're saying... then you hold in your hands an extremely powerful tool, one that can make a dramatic difference in creating an effective presentation.

But only if you read it and try the suggestions and approaches it offers.

Three simple techniques and one core concept, One Idea per Slide, can make your slides – and your presentation – better immediately. These "tools" by themselves won't create great presentations, but they will help you create *effective* presentations quickly.

Other books speak to the design artistry you can develop within a PowerPoint™ presentation, or to improved speaking styles, or to becoming a technology wiz with PowerPoint, or to persuasion techniques. This one speaks directly to turning awful, bullet-point-laden, sleep-inducing slides – *ordinary* slides – into successful, easy-to-create power tools that support the most important element of your presentation: you.

If you want to deliver presentations that matter, that inform and convince and even move the audience, dig in.

Exchange
the BAD
for
BETTER.

PowerPoint Doesn't Suck.

Bad Presentations Do.

PowerPoint is a tool. So's a hammer, whether used to erect wonderful buildings… or smash their walls.

There are good ways to hammer nails, and bad ways. A carpenter uses leverage rather than force to make hammering easy and effective. Likewise, you can learn to leverage PowerPoint to make your presentations effective — and easy.

"Death by PowerPoint"

It's unclear who first coined this phrase in the mid-2000s, but it caught on rapidly.

And why not? It's descriptive, only slightly exaggerated, and immediately recognizable by anyone who's ever sat through boring slides supported by a dull presenter.

Wait…. Aren't the slides supposed to support the presenter, and not the other way around?

Absolutely. And therein lies one of the keys to deadly presentations – somebody yapping away while we're squinting at the info on the slides.

Scenes From Deadly Presentations

Do you recognize any of these scenes?

- Slides filled with information… read aloud by the presenter… haltingly, slower than you can read for yourself. Extra credit if the presenter keeps turning her back to you to stare at her slides.
- The speaker drones on, often in a monotone.
- The audience quickly reads the slide, then checks smartphones. After the tenth slide, they no longer bother reading. After the fifteenth, they're done with email and are on to *Words With Friends*.
- The slides are filled with cascading bullet points that end in a font too small to read. Extra credit if the speaker apologizes for the size.

Plus: You owe it to the audience to engage them. You owe it to yourself to communicate your message.

- The audience pays more attention to the handout than the speaker.
- *You* have been the speaker in one of these scenes.

You Can Do Better

It doesn't matter how bad a speaker you believe you are. I know you can do better.

How do I know? Because you've opened this book and have at least glanced at this page. Even if you just found the book in your office and are wondering how it got there, by actually opening it and reading a few words, you have expressed a perhaps hidden desire to become…

Ah, what do I know? I'm not a psychologist.

Still, when we get up in front of people to speak, we naturally want to be effective. To make our points. To move them toward action, or toward our way of thinking. Or at least, not put them to sleep, not make them regret the time we're taking from them.

There are lots of ways to improve as a speaker and presenter. If you're using presentation software (PowerPoint, Keynote, etc.), the easist gains – the low-hanging fruit – come from improving the presentation itself. And one side effect of better presentations is that you become a better speaker.

Does This Apply Only to PowerPoint?

No! I use PowerPoint as a point of reference, and because it's by far the most popular presentation program. But other than a few tips in later chapters regarding specific PowerPoint menus and such, this book applies equally to Google Slides™, Prezi™, Apple Keynote™, Microsoft Sway™, and similar tools.

Death by speaking!
William Shakespeare, *Henry VI pt. 1*

What This Book Can (and Can't) Do for You

By itself, this book can't make you a more effective speaker. (Technically, that's not quite true. If you're a don't-move-while-you-grip-the-lectern speaker, you can put it on the floor and stand on it. You'll appear a bit taller. You're welcome.)

Hate Introductions?

If you hate introductions, whys and such, jump directly to p. 38.

A Word-Heavy *Book* About a Visual Tool?

What good is a book full of text when discussing a visual tool? Especially when the book is focused on creating better visual material? And when it doesn't even have a ton of pictures and visual examples?

Because "pretty" slides are not a useful end in themselves. "Slide cleanup" is for most decks a new paint job on a car with a blown engine. And creating beautiful slides is a lot of work. That work can pay off… but first you need to create slides that matter to your audience. And that task is not necessarily a visual, "artistic" effort.

Becoming a Better Speaker

This book is not about becoming a better speaker per se. There are plenty of tomes out there on that topic. If you're looking for specific speaking tips *out of context*, you won't find them here.

> **Plus:** There is no one-size-fits-all recipe. The approach in this book will help, not change the world by itself.

However, within the context of slides that connect with your audience, you'll find a wealth of suggestions that will help you improve both as a presenter (with slides) and a speaker (with or without slides). Many of the ideas in this book help you dispense with old habits that *get in your way* as a speaker.

My goal is to show you how to make your audience focus on your meaning and intent instead of tuning you out.

Bad slides lead to tune-outs. Your slides can and should help you communicate your key messages – and if you follow my suggestions, your slides may appear simple, but they won't be boring in context.

As you learn to communicate through a combination of effective slides and improved presentations driven by those slides, you'll feel better about presenting... and about reaching your audience, whether an auditorium full of people or half a dozen folks in a conference room.

Sure, you could commit to full-on presentation training – if you want to be a full-time speaker. But most of us just need some help in one aspect of our real job: when we have to present to a group.

What I offer is a lot simpler than time-consuming deep training, yet can yield many of the same benefits.

Changing your presentation materials and approach is the easiest and most efficient way to communicate more clearly.

Changing your materials also changes your presentation style. You'll engage with the audience over your content, not feed it to them (to which they normally react the way a cat does to being fed dry dog food).

Let me have audience for a word or two.
William Shakespeare, *As You Like It*

People Cannot Read and Listen Together

I trust you don't text while driving. You know it's dangerous.

People do not multitask. (See my book *The Off Switch* for more details, including various scientific studies and experiments.) When we face two tasks that require conscious attention, we context-switch: spend some time on Task A, put it aside, spend time on Task B, put *it* aside, try to remember where we were on Task A, and only then do we continue on that task.

We fool ourselves – sometimes – into believing we're doing two things at once, and that we're thus being more efficient. We're wrong on both counts. Numerous studies prove we'd accomplish more if we stuck to Task A for some time before allowing anything short of the fire alarm to interrupt us, giving no attention to Task B until we're ready to shine the full light of our attention on it.

Why does multitasking matter in the context of presenting?

Because bad presenters ask the audience to multitask. They present a slide dense with information while they talk. And reading + listening = multitasking… which we don't do so well. The words on the slide are brightly lit and new, so our attention goes to the slide. We tune the speaker out for a while.

Not good. Especially if you're the speaker.

If all you want is for them to read your stuff, email it and save everyone lots of time. People read faster than you speak, and most people absorb complex information better by reading it.

Plus: You're not a speaker. You're a guide. Reading (or competing with) your slides is ineffective guidework.

However, they usually comprehend it better and are more moved to act on it when it forms part of an interactive discussion led by a knowledgeable speaker.

That's why you're in front of the room. *You* are the guide to what matters, how it applies, how it fits within various contexts, what it looks like not on paper but in the messy real world. If you have slides full of words ("bullet points"), you'll struggle to connect – whether the audience reads them, you read to the audience, or you compete with your slides.

What If You're a Not-Very-Good Speaker?

Great speakers don't need visual aids to communicate. The Gettysburg Address. Roosevelt's fireside chats. Kennedy, Reagan, Clinton. No visuals, just words. If you're that good, that effective…. Well, most of us are not. And we rarely have that level of compelling material. (Or speechwriters. Or years of practice.)

If the rest of us want to move an audience, want them to retain information, we need to use all the tools at our disposal. We need to "present" rather than "speak." If you mumble, mutter, stare at your shoes, and refuse to communicate without reading from a prepared statement, this book alone can't change that. So let's assume you can be heard (or have a microphone), are willing to look at the audience once in a while, and have a desire to communicate with them (whether with information or to affect their thinking). With that as a baseline, and one other criterion, you're ready to become an effective presenter.

The remaining criterion?

You know more about your subject than the audience does. You hold that magic coin. You're the expert, at least as far as right-now, right-here in the presentation room. You've got something they want. That alone gives them reason to listen to you.

Tire the hearer with a book of words.
William Shakespeare, *Much Ado About Nothing*

Why Are You Presenting?

- ✓ It's good for your career.
- ✓ Your boss told you to.
- ✓ You have information your audience wants.
- ✓ You want to affect your audience's thinking on some issue.
- ✓ You like to hear yourself talk.

Most of these are good reasons to present material to an audience. (Just because the first two are "artificial" doesn't mean they're invalid.) And for all of them – even the cynical final element of the list – a more effective presentation will yield better results.

Let's focus on the third and fourth items, because even the first two really come down to #3 and #4.

Sharing Information

One of the two main purposes of presenting is to give the audience information they may currently lack.

However, if you just want to lay an "information dump" on your audience, why are you presenting? Send them your slides, or a position-paper document. But… if you want them to engage with the material, probe it, consider it, and ask you questions about it, a presentation is the way to go.

To be effective, though, that presentation must consist of something other than you standing near the screen, reading the slides.

Plus: Even information-dense presentations work better when you engage/connect with the audience.

Note that even many information-heavy presentations also include an element of "moving the audience," seeking to affect the way they think about a particular topic.

Teaching, especially at the high school level and above, represents a special case of information-sharing. You want the audience not only to gain information but to be able to retain and call upon it – and good teachers want them to process, respond to, and enlarge upon the content.

Moving Your Audience

Often, when we present, we want our audience to "do something" regarding our topic. We want to move them to a specific outlook on that topic from their previous view (or no view).

The hidden secret of effective presenters is that they always have such a goal, no matter how much or how little information they pass along. *You* have a view, an outlook, even if your view is, "It's important to know this stuff." The more committed you become to connecting with the audience over that view, the more likely that they'll come to share it – and will be engaged rather than bored.

Make-a-decision presentations, common in a business context, are a variant on moving the audience. You're presenting a small number of alternatives – traditionally, two or three – and asking the audience to select the best direction. See p. 130 for more.

Telling Your Story

Most great presentations tell stories – a single story, or a sequence of related stories. Restructuring your presentation is beyond the scope of this book. However, the final chapter offers a brief summary of one technique I find both easy and effective (p. 187).

I remember the story.
William Shakespeare, *The Tempest*

Five Takeaways

1. PowerPoint is neither the problem nor the solution. It's a tool. This book will help you learn to use it to support (not supplant) your material – and you.

2. People cannot multitask. They only task-switch, and do it badly. When you're up in front of them, they cannot listen to you and read your slides at the same time. Which do you want them to do?

3. Presentations have two purposes – convey information and/or change audience thinking. The latter is more powerful and has a more lasting effect.

4. The best presentations are "active," engaging the audience in two-way conversation – even if that "conversation" is one an attendee has with his or her previous way of considering your issue.

5. It's not about slide templates, but about communication. Templates at best keep you from tripping over your own feet, but they cannot set you on the right road, heading in the right direction.

Next Steps/Action Items

- Consider the most awful presentations you've sat through in the past year. Why were they awful?

- Try to attend a slide-based presentation in the next week or so that has little to do with your job – so you can focus on the presenter and not the content. What does she do well? What does she do poorly? How does the audience react? Where are they restless? Where are they focused?

Exchange the bad for better.
William Shakespeare, *Two Gentlemen of Verona*

Things
that are PAST
are DONE.

SET ASIDE
THE PAST.

DO THE SAME THING,
EXPECT DIFFERENT RESULTS?

Here are some things worth setting aside:

- *Your preconceptions on how to present.*
- *Your fears.*
- *Your existing slides.*

This chapter shows you how, and why that will help you succeed.

Why Bullet Points?

Why does a new PowerPoint slide default to bullet points?

I asked a colleague on the PowerPoint team that question a dozen years ago. He answered it with a question of his own: "What should it start with instead?"

A blank page, like word processing programs? Intimidating to many, more so in a presentation program whose users may be uncomfortable with the act of presenting. Modern versions of PowerPoint offer a (stark) title page first... and then give you bullet points when you click New Slide.

At any rate, just because the software offers up bullet points doesn't mean you need to use them.

"But We Think in Bullet Points...."

True, sort of.

We do tend to organize our thoughts in an outline fashion, and bullet points are a kind of outline, albeit one without numbers or letters.

But we don't submit our outlines as finished papers. We mold and shape them into the content we want readers to consume.

The same holds true for PowerPoint.

Plus: Bullet points are not the problem per se, but they exacerbate the profound issues of bad presentations.

Our outline is for our own use. We don't need to share it with the audience. An actor doesn't declaim the stage directions during a performance. (Except in *Macbeth*.) A poet doesn't share all the not-quite-so-good words she discarded in favor of the perfect one.

Presenting your ideas as bullet points does the audience a disservice, offering them sketches of your ideas instead of the ideas themselves. The presenter with nothing more to offer than a handful of bullet point might as well email a short memo.

(Some of you are thinking, "Yeah, that would be easier. But my boss says I have to give this presentation." Assume your boss isn't just looking to embarrass you, but rather believes you have something to offer. You know more about the subject than your audience – not just the outlines, but the subtleties, the nuances, the myriad factors that can make even the driest subject come alive. I've sat through engaging presentations on actuarial tables, text searches, traffic data, and the properties of rubber at low temperatures. The content mattered to the speaker, who then made it matter to us. I've also sat through stone boring presentations on some of what should have been the most exciting topics imaginable, all of which stifled that excitement within bullet points.)

I'm not afraid to use bullet points when I'm outlining a presentation, but they're gone by the time I'm finished with the design stage.

Don't confuse bullet points – the presentation style – with an unnumbered list whose items are set off by text bullets, such as the lists of Action Items that end most chapters in this book (e.g., p. 15). That said, I'll describe interesting alternative ways to present unnumbered lists starting on pp. 88 and 150.

Ring the bell.
William Shakespeare, *Macbeth* (a direction to the stage manager accidentally copied into Macduff's dialog, and now part of the standard text of the play)

The "Standard" Presentation

Look at the first example of a deadly presentation, the IT budget request on p. 26. It's a bit exaggerated, but only a bit. In fact, it's quite similar to dozens of presentations I've sat through in the corporate world. Many such projects went unfunded, some deservedly because they showed little ROI (return on investment), but a significant number because they were presented so badly.

So what's wrong with the presentation?

Surface Errors

The presentation's verbose. It's badly formatted. It's full of jargon (e.g., "sourcing" is meaningful in HR, not so meaningful to the CFO or controller). The template doesn't really support the material. Slide 5 runs past the bottom of the working area and into the footer – and is almost incomprehensible even for someone who works in IT, let alone the rep from the CFO's office. The type on some of the slides is unreadable on screen (though I presume the people in the meeting have hard copies of the spreadsheet from slide 6). In fact, there are at least a dozen "mechanical" errors on these slides.

But fixing them before you address the deeper issues is putting lipstick on the pig.

What's Really Wrong

First, there's no message. No story. No purpose.

> **Plus:** Surface errors are "clean-up" – worth doing, but not game-changing. Fix the real problems first.

Second, there's no "there" there (cf. Gertrude Stein). It's a bunch of disconnected stuff – some facts, some opinions, some opinions masquerading as facts. What do you want the audience to *do* when the presentation is done? (Right. Approve funding for the project. Based on the material in the slides, why would they do that?)

Third, what's the "hook" for the intended audience? For that matter, can you tell who the intended audience is? The slides aren't exactly speaking the language of someone representing the company's fiscal interests. Psst – "numbers people" making multi-million-dollar decisions are interested in more than numbers. (Oh, and they'll probably spot the errors on the spreadsheet, too!)

Fourth, the audience's attention will be split, at first between the slides and the speaker, then among the slides, the speaker, and their email. I'll bet by the end of the presentation, their email wins out. Which isn't good for the speaker… or the funding request. It's fine for the audience's attention to go to the spreadsheet when you start digging into the numbers, but by then it'll be too late for this project – because you haven't given them reason to commit to it, to believe that it will benefit the company. So they'll nitpick the numbers, which are always nitpickable, and the funding request will likely fail unless a) the competing requests are equally disjointed or b) there's been behind-the-scenes politicking.

Fith, it's downright ugly. All the surface errors summarized on the opposite page will indeed take their toll. So you do need to fix them. But fixing them won't "move the needle" until you address the larger problem.

By the way, one bit of good news: once you've adopted the recommended methods, you'll have a lot less text, with far fewer surface errors that need fixing.

Quips and sentences, and these paper bullets.
William Shakespeare, *Much Ado About Nothing*

Set Aside Your Preconceptions on PowerPoint

"PowerPoint Tells You to Use Bullet Points"

PowerPoint offers bullet points as the default. So why should you do what I suggest, rather than use PowerPoint "as is"?

Microsoft Word™ offers a blank page as the default. Does that mean you should never write anything? Or never format it?

Bullet points are the default in part for historical reasons, ever since 1987, when Microsoft bought the company that first developed PowerPoint. Bullet points do provide novices something of a starting point. And… they're easy. Maybe.

"Bullet Points Are Easy"

Easy for whom? Not for your audience.

Bullet points are like underwear. They're a useful outlining tool as you structure and assemble your presentation (p. 18, e.g.). But they shouldn't be visible in the final product, your presentation.

Only Madonna presents in her underwear – and even she hasn't done that for years.

Plus: PowerPoint is a flexible tool that *you* control. Don't let the *tool* dictate your presentation style.

"The Audience Needs Detail"

Some audiences need detail for some aspects of some presentations. Words on slides are a particularly poor way to convey such detail. Use handouts (p. 164) – e.g., the costs spreadsheet in the IT Budget "bad example" on p. 30. It's fine for a slide to duplicate the handout as a placeholder while you're discussing the detail – but that's only one aspect of a presentation.

See also the spreads on presenting scientific papers (p. 126) and teaching dense content (p. 128).

"The Audience Wants Flashy Stuff"

The audience wants cool animations. Flying transitions. Zooms and sounds and lions and tigers and bears. Oh my.

No. They don't. Some animations are useful in helping you make a point (p. 98). Most don't do much, and some are downright counterproductive. Transitions between slides (p. 114) are worse. Don't sweat them, at least for now.

"PowerPoint Is Hard to Learn and I Don't Have Time"

That's not unreasonable. But you can make huge strides and master these quick fixes without moving much beyond the novice level. This book covers everything you need to know.

PowerPoint is an incredibly flexible and powerful tool once you get past the default bullet-point layout. You don't have to become a PowerPoint wizard to gain access to a significant portion of this power – because it comes not from menu options but from the way you structure your presentation and your slides.

Bullets! I'll drink more than will do me good.
William Shakespeare, *Henry IV pt. 2*

Set Aside Your Fears – and Your Preconceptions on Presenting

"I'm Not Good at Presenting"

Few people are, without practice.

Here are some data points to consider:

1. Each time you present, you learn. You get better.

2. Saddling yourself with a Death-by-PowerPoint presentation puts you in an uphill battle from the getgo. Doing the same-old-same-old and expecting different results is the definition of insanity.

3. One Idea per Slide puts the emphasis where it belongs, on communicating your material and informing/moving the audience.

4. This book contains lots of tips for becoming better at presenting, even though it's not a presentation-tips book per se. Even the best actors fail in bad movies. Assemble better ~~movies~~ presentations and your presentation effectiveness will increase

5. I've devoted an entire spread to the I'll-forget-what-I'm-going-to-say trap (p. 44).

Plus: Don't compare yourself to professional or top-flight presenters. Focus instead on telling your story.

6. The perfect is the enemy of the good. Don't worry about not being great at presenting. Instead, focus on the very achievable goals of a) being better than you were last week and b) communicating your material more effectively. In fact, the more you focus on the latter, the less you'll worry about the former – and the easier it will be to beat last week's standard.

"I'm Afraid I'll Look Stupid"

Serving up Death by PowerPoint won't do wonders for perceptions of your IQ.

So don't.

Instead, play to your strengths. You're the expert on your material. Use these suggestions and the core One Idea per Slide to reinforce rather than undercut your capabilities.

"People Just Want the Facts"

You believe the world looks like Sgt. Joe Friday's "Just the facts, ma'am"? Then write up those facts and send copies in email. Indeed, some attendees *do* just want the facts, written out. Reading them on your slides, a laborious process, won't make them happy.

Once you commit (or someone commits you) to a presentation, however, you need to focus on the communications approach you do have – live interaction – rather than one you might wish you had. (Or do both. Send a written document in advance, for those who will read it. Then forget about it and focus on the communications modality at hand, the presentation.)

Show them entertainment.
William Shakespeare, *Timon of Athens*

Set Aside Your Existing Slides

If your existing slides have bullet points, lots of text, full sentences, and more than One Idea per Slide, set them aside.

We're going to do something different.

Something new.

And – though I suspect you won't accept this yet – something easier.

You'll spend a bit longer in slide preparation – not because the PowerPoint design aspects are harder (they're easier, in fact), but because you'll take more time to think about the material itself – structure, context, story, purpose, etc.

And the actual presentation will be easier as well. You'll be less anxious. You'll be more focused on communication and results, rather than surviving the time allotted. You'll build connection with the audience, increasing the likelihood you'll achieve your goals, some combination of informing them (rather than simply telling them stuff), moving them/changing their thinking on some issue, and/or making your boss happy.

(I'm not dismissing the importance of that last item. Few managers want you to fail, because it makes them look bad as well.)

Your Current Slides

If you give presentations regularly, e.g., as a teacher, a speaker, etc., you probably have a set of "stock" slides you draw on.

Plus: Set your current slides aside for now. You'll draw on them later.

However, chances are your current slides resemble the "bad example" decks (p. 30 ff.) to at least some degree. So set them aside. (For now.)

You won't find much help here on fixing them, per se. That's slide clean-up (pp. 20 and 199), surface errors. If your patient has a broken leg and a small cut on her elbow, you need to focus on the splint, not the Band-Aid®.

I'm not disparaging the Band-Aid. You need to keep the cut clean, let it heal without infection. But the cut is not your first priority.

Your existing slides contain a lot of material, and you'll use that material as you develop a more effective deck. The material, but not necessarily the slides themselves.

First, much of the content of the slides should be spoken rather than "simulcast" (presented onscreen and paraphrased by you).

Second, you likely have more than One Idea per Slide, and we're going to simplify and focus. (Multiple ideas per slide have a few specific applications, such as summaries and discussions, and we'll deal with those in a later chapter, on p. 70.)

None of that existing content is going to waste. It's all useful, even necessary. If you're speaking on the same topic, you'll reuse that material.

However, you won't necessarily use it in its current visual form. It will inform your presentation. It will support your points, your theses. It will matter to you, and to those who hear you present.

There are more ways to communicate than simply having the audience read your slides.

Our purposed hunting shall be set aside.
William Shakespeare, *A Midsummer Night's Dream*

Set Aside All the Bad Presentations You've Given

Were they great? Did you feel good about them?

Either way, they're in the past. That's not an address we wish to claim as our residence.

This Page Intentionally

Plus: You remember what you did last week. Your audience remembers what *they* (not you) did last week.

Left Blank. (Mostly.)

So you're failed in the past.

So what?

It's a new day, and all that. No one cares, or remembers, what happened in the past. (Except you. And you probably exaggerate it, making both the successes and the failures more memorable than they actually were for the others who were there.)

Will you with counters sum the past?
William Shakespeare, *Troilus and Cressida*

Bad Example #1: IT Budget

IT Budget Meeting
Project Reindeer Funding Request
November 16, 2016

Project Reindeer Agenda

- Project Description
- Why we need this project
- Costs
- Timeline
- Summary

Project Description

- Source candidates from a larger pool
- User population
  - 38 external recruiters
    - "Headhunters"
  - 21 internal recruiters
  - 346 HR generalists and specialists
  - Hiring managers worldwide
- 4500 hires annually
- Project delivery: 14 months

Why we need this project

- Lack of coordination among internal recruiters, external recruiters (headhunters), HR team, and hiring managers
- Sourcing candidates mostly from traditional sources
  - Missing out on new media
  - Missing population of candidates
    - Entry level
    - Spot hires
    - Middle manager return-to-workforce
- Duplication of efforts
- Discoordinated contact with candidates

Amalgamated Ruminants Ltd.
Voted *Best IT Dept. in Class*

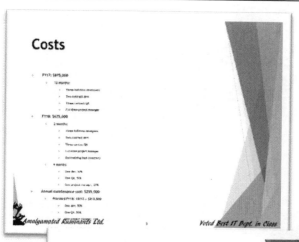

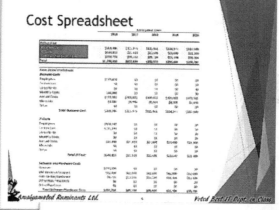

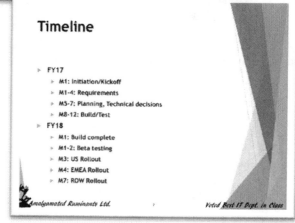

Bad Example #2: Conference Paper

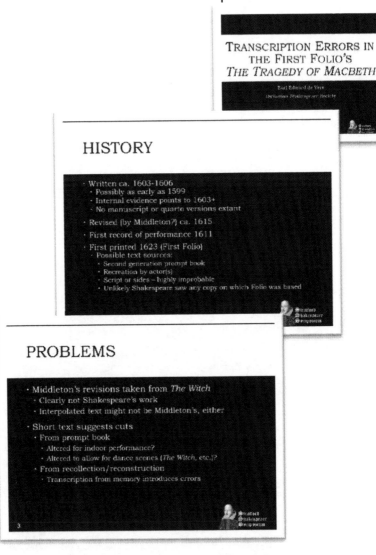

GOT "MILK"?

$$x \; / \; x \; / \; x \; / \; x \; / \; x \; / \; x$$
It is too full o'the milk of human kindness
$$x \; / \; x \; / \; x \; /$$
To catch the nearest way....

- Extra syllable
  - 11 beats is not unknown, but particularly awkward here
- What is "the milk of human kindness"?
  - And what does it have to do with greed and ambition?
- Consider instead "the milk of humankind"
  - Makes sense, both large and small
  - Fits with other Lady Macbeth images:
    - "Pour my spirits"
    - "To love the babe that milks me"

4

NOW RING THE BELL!

Ring the alarum bell! Murder and treason!
(five more lines)
To countenance this horror. Ring the bell.

- Why does Macduff command this twice?
  - The Porter might be drunk, but the time for comedy is over
- Stage directions always phrased as imperatives in prompt-books
- If the bell started ringing when first requested, it would drown out the rest of Macduff's speech
- So, Mr. Stage Manager, he's done, so ring the bell to cement the moment

5

Five Takeaways

1. The default PowerPoint layout of nested bullet points is useful for outlining your message while you're preparing your presentation – not for communicating that message.

2. PowerPoint is an incredibly flexible and powerful tool once you get past the default bullet-point layout. And you don't have to become a PowerPoint wizard to gain access to a significant portion of this power, because it comes not from menu options but from the way you structure your presentation and your slides.

3. Don't let your preconceptions or fears about presenting trap you into giving standard-but-ineffective presentations. You're capable of more. Your audience deserves better – and so do you.

4. Your current store of slides probably contains useful content. You can reuse the content itself even as you redesign and restructure the actual slides.

5. The fastest and easiest way to improve as a presenter is to improve the presentations themselves.

Next Steps/Action Items

- Pick a presentation to which you'll apply the techniques and tips of this book:

  - o An upcoming presentation is best if you're not under time pressure. Don't try to apply these techniques to tomorrow's lecture. This approach is not in itself time-consuming, but new ideas need to percolate. Leave time to absorb the concept rather than trying to treat it like disconnected rules.
  - o Rework an old presentation.
  - o Fix whichever one of the bad examples comes closest to the kinds of presentations you normally give.
  - o Or create a new presentation you've always wanted to deliver. You may never show it to anyone, but it's a great way to break through old habits and barriers because you'll have little to no delivery anxiety.

- Open PowerPoint (or whatever presentation program you're using) and actually apply these steps, at least to parts of your presentation. Reading about One Idea per Slide and applying in in your mind's eye is not enough. It's fine to read (or skim) the next three chapters before digging in – but then go back and apply them to actual slides.

- Don't give up, even if what I'm suggesting seems radically different from everything else you've ever done. Unless your current approach is working great, why not dare to be better – better than you have been, and frankly better than your peers? (And then inspire your peers/colleagues to become better as well.)

Things that are past are done.
William Shakespeare, *Antony and Cleopatra*

FIX YOUR SLIDES NOW

This section defines the core ideas of the so-called quick fix (and I suppose I'm the one so-calling it, since the working title of this book was *PowerPoint Quick-Fix Guide*). Recognize that you, not your slides, must be the focus of the presentation, then focus your presentation into One Idea per Slide, with each slide having a specific purpose within the context of your presentation and your overall goals.

Why do I call it a quick fix? Well, it won't take too long, and it will fix your slides, but… "quick fix" is sort of pejorative.

There are a number of all-encompassing approaches to creating excellent presentations. Some are terrific, but they require you to buy into their approach fully. Stick with them, and you'll probably see significant improvement over time.

But that's the final 20%, going from good to great. What about the middle 60%, going from bad to good?

Turns out that one of the biggest problems in Death by PowerPoint is simple: terrible slides. Slides that conflict with the presenter. Slides that draw focus away. Slides that bore the audience to sleep or to email or to contagious inattention.

Those are problems you can fix quickly.

Let's get to work.

First, Define Success

Any project should start with a definition of success, a goal that is clear, achievable (possible), and available (meaning that you control the major factors in reaching it).

How will you define success for each presentation?

Presentations That Move the Audience to Action

Bad Example #1 (p. 30), funding an IT project, needs to move the audience. However, "Get the project funded" is probably not available. If you propose a great project, two other teams propose even higher-return projects, and there is funding for only two projects, you'll fail to get funded no matter what you do. A more reasonable goal might be: "CFO believes project is worth funding."

Note how the existence of that goal by itself forces changes in the presentation. What percentage of the content on the current slide deck speaks to that goal? Maybe 25% at best. A lot of words describe the project (in a combination of HR- and IT-speak). There's some stuff about the user population, though little about how the new tool will make their lives better. There's not much about how it benefits the company, and what *is* there is implied rather than clear. There's a spreadsheet full of financial numbers… but it's all about costs, not what you get in return for those costs. Sure, the CFO could read into all of that to figure out the value, or question you directly, and in fact she's probably quite used to doing so… but why not make her life easier? Your job is to change her thinking, not present a bunch of stuff and hope she catches on.

These types of presentations usually have clear goals. Find them.

Plus: The Cheshire Cat pointed out that if you don't know where you're going, all roads are the same.

Presentations That Impart Information

It's easier to set goals for presentations that move the audience. Information sessions are harder, especially in the absence of tests of knowledge.

Consider the conference session that forms Bad Example #2 (p. 32). Is your goal to inform the audience? (Half of them don't care about Shakespeare, and many are sitting through your presentation awaiting the chance to give their own.) Is it to boost your CV on the road to full professorship? (That's legitimate, though you should develop a presentation-related goal as well.)

This Bad Example, like the preceding one, meanders. It's an information-dump: "I know some stuff and I'm going to tell you about it." Unless the audience is already interested in the particular bit of arcana you're about to share, they won't care.

But what about, "Help them teach Shakespeare more effectively by recognizing that some of the things that don't make sense are actually mistakes"? Or, "Make productions of Macbeth better by getting closer to what Shakespeare actually wrote"? Or even, "Let's enjoy the genius of Shakespeare by laughing together at Middleton's emendations"?

If your goal is to impart information, focus your efforts not on the information itself but on the information *transfer*.

Adding a Personal Secondary Goal

Consider adding a goal that relates to your own growth as a presenter: Trying out One Idea per Slide (p. 58). Getting free of the lectern (p. 178). Actively engaging with the audience (p. 180). Using visual or image-based slides (p. 98). Enjoying the experience of presenting (or at least being a little less scared this time than last).

Dream of success and happy victory.
William Shakespeare, *Richard III*

Why should I NOT SUCCEED?

1. You Are the Focus.

Not Your Slides. Not Your Words. You.

Wait. You say you just want to fix your slides, not your presentation style? The biggest problem with most slides is that they prevent the audience from focusing on the presenter. And on the content she has to offer.

This book can't do much about your speaking abilities. (Other books and – better – interactive classes tackle that problem.) But it can help you keep bad slides from making your life much, much harder than it has to be.

Be Better Than an Email

Why do presenters put their content on their slides?

- They want to be sure their audience gets the information.
- They're worried they'll forget what they want to say.

This spread covers first point. I'll address the second in the following spread.

Why a Presentation?

The best medium for the simple communication of facts, data, and information in most cases is a document (a generic term that can include email, spreadsheets, PowerPoint decks designed to be read rather than projected, etc.). Readers can absorb the material at their own pace, go back and reread, skip sections that don't apply or don't interest them, etc. And we generally read faster than speakers talk.

Most of us supplanted being read to by about age six.

So why would a presenter read his slides aloud?

No, the reason we value presentations is that the presenter adds depth to the material. Trial lawyers don't hand their closing arguments to the jury, but deliver them with eye contact and passion. Great persuaders know that their presence matters at least as much as their words.

Plus: What a valuable gift you've been given, the audience's time. This chapter is about using it well.

Richard Feynman and the O-Rings

Testifying before Congress in the wake of the Challenger Space Shuttle disaster, physicist Richard Feynman bent a flexible O-ring and placed it in a cup of ice water as he spoke. Then he pulled it out and showed it failing to return to its flexible state. In a masterful bit of understatement, he noted, "I believe that has some significance for our problem."

Yes, indeed.

His demonstration had a far more memorable effect than his protestations in the Appendix to the Rogers Commission report.

That's why you present!

Of course, we may have few moments as dramatic as Feynman's testimony. Maybe we don't present on life-or-death issues. No matter. Our presence itself affords us the opportunity to reach the audience in ways words alone rarely can.

Take advantage of that opportunity.

Or at least stop letting your slides get in the way!

An effective presentation does not duplicate material best absorbed by reading. You can summarize it, or highlight particular aspects, or help the audience retain it via clear images, interaction, and more.

(Sometimes you do have to present "dense" material, and I offer a few spreads to help make those presentations effective as well on pp. 126 and 128. But even with such material, you'll have slides setting up the material, others summarizing key ideas, and so on. Also note the spreads on slides that show data, pp. 70 and 82.)

Whether you're presenting because you want to or because your boss told you to, don't "deliver the mail." Take charge of the interaction and lead the audience.

What say you to his expertness?
William Shakespeare, *All's Well That Ends Well*

Forgetting What You Want to Say

Most presenters worry, at the start of their "presentation career," that they'll forget what they want to say. Thus despite any desire to keep the slides simple and readable from the back row, they load them up with more and more points – bullet points – related to the heading of the slide.

In effect, they offer the audience their "presenter's notes."

When you pick up a book, do you want to read the author's finely crafted words, or his notes? The audience doesn't want to see *your* notes, either.

You say, "But I can't craft my spoken words the way an author can." Perhaps. But bullet-point notes aren't well crafted, either – and they're hard to read as well.

Presenter's Notes

PowerPoint's **Presenter View** is a powerful, underappreciated tool that I explore further on p. 176. Among other things, it allows you to project your slides on the big screen while showing you your notes on your laptop (or the monitor of the supplied computer in the presentation room).

Your notes! As in, all those points you wanted to make sure you touched on. You no longer need put them on the slide itself.

You may have to play around a bit to get them to fit, either by shortening them or adjusting the **Presenter View** windows, but you're no longer without them.

Plus: One Idea per Slide minimizes the time you spend staring at your screen. Focus on the audience instead.

But while it's fine to put one or two key points – or a quote you want to make sure you repeat exactly – in the notes, there's a better way than jamming all your notes plus ideas onto one slide.

Simple Slides, Each With One Idea

The best slides are the simplest, each with one, single idea.

Sometimes the idea is expressed in a few words. Sometimes it's a picture, with or without words. Sometimes it's a diagram – the less complicated, the better.

But it's never a bunch of bullet points vying for the audience's focus. That focus belongs on you. (Occasionally it belongs on the data, or on other audience members, as I'll discuss in the next chapter, but it almost never belongs on the *words* on your slide.)

Instead of one slide with five points, try five slides, each with one point. Or six, if you want to include a topic/header slide. Now you won't forget what you want to say next, because a summary (or hint or picture) appears on the next slide.

At first, this method appears to violate some unwritten (or badly written) rule, since you may wind up with 60+ slides per hour. But I guarantee you'll have far less "stuff" on those sixty slides than you would have had in a dozen, stuff that distracts and confuses and defocuses your audience.

So What If You Forget Something!

All presenters forget something from time to time.

It's okay. You're the only one who notices. We are never perfect.

I forgot to ask him one thing. I'll remember it anon.
William Shakespeare, *Cymbeline*

We Cannot Multitask

Don't text and drive.

Don't speak while your audience is reading.

Just… don't. Multitasking is for computers. (And even they don't actually multitask, but fake it by very rapid "context switching.")

Audiences Can Read…

Plus: For more on multitasking, see p. 10 and my book *The Off Switch*.

or Listen. Not Both.

Once you commit (or get committed) to a presentation, you're the focus. Not your slides.

Death by PowerPoint is in part the result of a focus conflict between busy slides and a live human being who's talking (or not) while the audience is trying to read.

Even the world's worst speaker – and your interest in this book suggests you're nowhere near that level – is hurt rather than helped by slides that compete with him. Stop reading, start talking with the audience, and stop making them read as well.

Scary?

I suppose. But is it any more scary than what's already happening?

Such welcome and unwelcome things at once.
William Shakespeare, *Macbeth*

"It's Scary Up There"

Yes, it is.

That's part of the nature of presentations. You're taking a risk.

You take a similar risk, of course, when you write a report and send it around. People may criticize it, pick at it, even mock the author. Except you're not around when they do it.

Or they may be bored, put it aside, pay it little attention.

When you present live to an audience, people may criticize you – but they rarely do so directly, in your presence. So it's no different than a report in that regard. Their boredom and inattention may be a bit more visible… but so is their engagement and enthusiasm.

And you have a change to change their attitude when they're there in front of you.

If You Really Hate Presenting...

This book can't make you love presenting if you're one of those people who prefer going to the dentist to speaking in front of a formally assembled group.

But y'know, sometimes the dentist pokes and prods and scrapes for a few minutes, then smiles and says, "No cavities this time." And sometimes the audience actually wants to be there, to listen to you and learn from you. If your boss is in effect dragging you to the rostrum, at least take it as a hopeful opportunity – and then use these methods to make it much less painful!

What are your other fears, beyond forgetting (p. 44)?

Plus: "Great" is hard. *Good* slides that will support you as the presenter are the proverbial low-hanging fruit.

Looking foolish: Coming in with a Death by PowerPoint deck won't make you look less foolish. Instead, offer clean slides that don't interfere with what you want to say. They needn't be elegant; choose a simple visual style, such as text-only, to start (p. 100).

Freezing: Remember that all your key ideas are still in the deck. While you can leave ideas off your slides in the One Idea per Slide format and then talk about them without specific slide backup, you can also include a slide for each idea you wish to communicate. These slides plus your goal for the presentation (p. 38) guide you to the start line and beyond. You're much less likely to freeze because each slide links logically to the next. Of course, the fear of freezing isn't about logic. But if you know you've mapped a clear pathway, walking that pathway gives you confidence that you won't freeze up.

Being Boring: You may be here – this page, this book – because presenting isn't optional. So your only choice is to find tools to make your presentation as un-boring as possible. "Death by PowerPoint" slides are the ultimate in boring. The next two chapters will help you create support materials that maximize the chance of clear communication – which is the opposite of boring.

Being Unprepared: Work on your slides using these methods and you won't be unprepared. Practice a few times, and you won't be under-prepared, either. Dumping thoughts into bullet points feels like preparation – until you get up in front of that audience and realize your presentation is a muddled mess. This book's approach allows you to prepare properly… without working harder.

Rejection: All of the above really come down to fear of rejection. I get it. That's very real, and I suffer from it as well. I *hate* rejection. But I love communicating, making a difference to my audience, more than I fear rejection. The feeling that I've helped someone – changed their mind, informed them, engaged them – totally blows away all thoughts of rejection.

I never stood on ceremonies, yet now they fright me.
William Shakespeare, *Julius Caesar*

Shrinking Attention Spans

I'm not going to bemoan shrinking attention spans, or even claim that this trope reflects truth rather than perception. But let's acknowledge some realities about presenting:

- Audience attention spans tend to be limited – not everyone, not all the time, but in aggregate.
- Opportunities for distraction abound – smart phones, e-readers, and more.
- People sometimes zone out, whether daydreaming or focusing on burning problems in a high-pressure society.
- Darkened rooms are conducive to projection screens… and to zoning out.

You as a presenter can either throw a self-pity party or seek ways to succeed in the face of these realities – and perhaps even turn a few to your advantage.

Distractions

Consider ways that audience members, when they feel antsy, might turn to your distractions rather than their own. For example, you can offer handouts that contain more than just copies of the slides (p. 167). Every opportunity for interaction – taking questions (p. 164), asking them (p. 180), or walking around, freeing yourself from the stage (p. 179) – breaks the rhythms of somnolence and engages the audience in *your* "distractions" rather than their own. Most importantly, simple, easy-to-read slides keep them focused on you – the One Idea per Slide decks that this book recommends.

> **Plus:** Distractions happen. What you *can* control is how you plan for and deal with them.

You can help your cause by creating slides whose sequence isn't a predictable rhythm. If every slide after your title slides has its own title above a series of bullet points full of lengthy text, complex ideas, and sub-bullets offering more of the same, your rhythm is as exciting as the drip from a leaky faucet. Vary your slides! This book offers ideas throughout, but see especially the chapter on Visual Styles and the spreads following p. 96.

Zoning Out

It is critical to offer those who drop out for a minute – whether they zone out, respond to an email, or leave to answer a call of nature or the siren song of caffeine – a way back into your presentation. Experienced speakers know how to do this, and they don't take such comings and goings personally. But even first-time speakers can structure their presentations to provide two types of signposts (p. 140):

1. Those that alert the audience in advance to the structure of the presentation.
2. Those that help the audience find their way back into the presentation after they've departed, mentally or physically, for a time.

Going Beyond Quick-Fix Ideas

All of the suggestions above, and many more throughout this book, fall within the quick-fix scope of our work. You can achieve them using only your (much improved) slides and simple adjustments to your presentation style to support those upgraded slides.

The rest come with experience, bolstered by some of the Suggested Readings (p. 212). But you can get, say, 80% of the benefit of these ideas from the first 20% of your efforts, by focusing on the suggestions here and discarding the old way of doing things.

I know not what 'twas but distraction.
William Shakespeare, *Twelfth Night*

You Matter

Why is the audience there?

To see and hear and learn from you. (Okay, maybe their bosses told them they had to come… but once they're in the room, they're there for you.)

They want you to be good.

They want you to succeed.

The Audience Wants You

Plus: When you're in the audience waiting, do you hope the speaker will fail? Of course not.

to Succeed.

It's simple. They want their time in the room to be useful. Thus they're actually on your side (the odd case of office politics aside). They want you to be good. Entertaining. Informative. Challenging.

The fastest way to fail is to present boring slides and read from them with low energy. That's Death by PowerPoint.

But you're not going to do that.

You're going to offer simple slides, clean, clear, and crisp, with One Idea per Slide, as detailed in the next chapter.

And because the slides contain few words and do not duplicate what you're saying, the audience will listen to you rather than fall asleep slogging through your slides.

So let's create those slides.

Give me leave to try success.
William Shakespeare, *All's Well That Ends Well*

Five Takeaways

1. Reading slides in a dark room is soporific. You're the focus. You.

2. Audiences cannot read and listen at the same time. If they're reading, they're not listening. And if they're reading your notes – see Takeaway #1 – they're bored. So…

3. Don't put your notes on screen. Summarize your ideas with at most a few onscreen words. Then speak to those ideas with your own words, your own subject-matter expertise.

4. One Idea per Slide.

5. The audience wants you to succeed. If you succeed, their day is improved.

Next Steps/Action Items

- Visualize yourself succeeding at a presentation. Athletes do this all the time. Watch Jordan Spieth standing over a putt, or Steven Nash at the free-throw line. They see the ball going in the hole (larger ball, larger hole in Nash's case). See yourself delivering in front of an audience.

- Pick a deck to build or fix, ideally one for an upcoming presentation. That's what you'll work on in the next two chapters.

Why should I not succeed?
William Shakespeare, *Henry VI pt. 3*

Being
the RIGHT
IDEA.

2. ONE IDEA PER SLIDE.

ONE IDEA, LARGE OR SMALL. WITH ROOM TO BREATHE.

PowerPoint lets you smush all sorts of stuff onto a single slide, in type that resembles the bottom row of the eye chart.

And why not? Too often, the rest of the text makes as much sense as the eye chart text. E F P T O Z ThisIdea ThatThought AndAnotherThing.

Don't test the audience's visual acuity. Or their concentration acuity. Stick to One Idea per Slide.

Focus: One Idea per Slide

Your slides are supposed to support you – your thoughts, your concepts, your story, your message.

You can say only one thing at a time.

Therefore, why would you try to have multiple things on a given slide? Where does your audience's attention go? To reading the slide, first of all. (While you're talking, which annoys them.) Then, each time your voice or manner suggests you might be shifting to the next point, their attention returns to the screen to find that point – and again drifts away from the main focus, you.

So the first big trick to improving your slides dramatically is to avoid stuffing each slide full. One slide, one idea. One clear purpose as well, which is the subject of the next chapter (p. 75).

(There are a few exceptions, which I'll cover in a later spread, p. 70.)

There are two basic approaches to molding content into a One Idea per Slide presentation.

Leave Supporting Points off the Slide

A typical Death by PowerPoint slide contains a slide title summarizing the idea followed by a series of (nested) bullet points.

Plus: Keep the audience's attention on you *and* your material by sticking to One Idea per Slide.

HISTORY

- Written ca. 1603-1606
  - Possibly as early as 1599
  - Internal evidence points to 1603+
  - No manuscript or quarto versions extant
- Revised (by Middleton?) ca. 1615
- First record of performance 1611
- First printed 1623 (First Folio)
  - Possible text sources:
    - Second generation prompt book
    - Recreation by actor(s)
    - Script or sides – highly improbable
    - Unlikely Shakespeare saw any copy on which F

Here's a slide from a conference lecture on *Macbeth*, taken from Bad Example #2 (p. 32). Since the real subject is textual errors, the bulk of this slide is background info. You're setting up the meat of the presentation.

So why not get rid of the detail, period? How about just the years 1603, 1615, and 1623, big numbers, right in the middle of the slide?

Now the audience is intrigued. Most will guess the first and last (Shakespeareans know the date of the First Folio), but 1615 will have most of them guessing – and hanging on your words. Few think Middleton's doggerel adds much to the play. When you note what that year means in this context, you'll see a lot of positive head nodding. They're on your side – and you haven't even gotten to your main point yet.

Use Multiple Slides

If this slide instead were for a classroom session about the play's history, I might divide it into multiple slides:

- Authorship.
- First performance.
- Middleton.
- First Folio.
- Possible sources (separated from the march of dates).

Using this example, I'll show various approaches to One Idea per Slide might in the next few spreads.

Perilous stuff which weighs upon the heart.
William Shakespeare, *Macbeth*

Example: Conference Lecture/Seminar

On the preceding page I described how I'd convert the History slide of Bad Example #2 into the One Idea per Slide format.

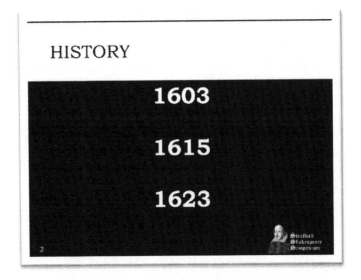

Here's a simple version, with no attempt to improve the format, dispense with the silly template logo, change the typeface, etc.:

- I typed the dates with an extra line between each one
- I enlarged the font by clicking the **Font/Increase the Font Size** button (**A^**) a few times.
- I removed the bullets by clicking the **Bullets** button in the **Paragraph** tab of the **Home** menu.
- I centered the text via the **Paragraph/Center** button.

Plus: These revised slides are not necessarily gorgeous. They're simple, and functional, and clean.

If I wanted to tinker more, I'd move the text box down, away from the white title box, and I'd get rid of the *)(@&!^ conference logo (p. 116), but this will do for now... and it took about fifteen seconds. (Even if it takes you longer, you'll still spend less time than typing and proofreading those lengthy bullet points!)

Speaking to This Slide

Since the audience is no longer reading the slide, I not only need to make the key points myself, I have total freedom as to how I want to present them.

For example, perhaps I assumed, going in, that my attendees represented a broad swath of literature knowledge, only to discover that everyone attending my session was a Shakespearean scholar. Great! Now I don't need to go into the history. I might say instead, "You probably recognize 1623 as the date of the First Folio and 1603 as the most likely authorship date. What happened around 1615?" People will call out a few things, until somebody in this population guesses Middleton – or even starts reciting Hecate's lines (see the quote at the bottom of this page).

On the other hand, if it turns out I do have a more general audience, I'll spend a bit of time filling in the information behind the dates – the same facts stuffed into the bullet points on the original (preceding spread).

My laptop/monitor notes page might include, at most, the first three sub-bullets – information that's both minor and exacting. If I speak to this level of detail, I want to be sure I get it right. (Since the entire presentation is about textual errors, I-as-lecturer probably know enough about the last main item, the ways that errors could have crept into the text, to fully bore anyone for fifteen minutes without notes.)

Oh, well done. I commend your pains.
~~William Shakespeare~~ Thomas Middleton, *Macbeth*

Example: Information Session (Classroom)

On p. 59 I suggested breaking the Bad Example #2 History slide into multiple slides if you needed the audience to concentrate on the details, maybe along these lines:

WRITTEN

FIRST PERFORMANCE

HERE COMES MIDDLETON

PRINTED

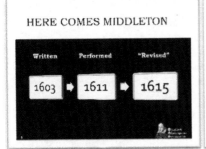

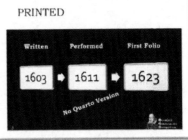

I used **Smart Art** to create the boxes, then **Design/Styles** to add perspective (specifically **Metallic Scene**, which adds a 3D look). I then typed the annotation text ("Earliest," "Probable," etc.) into **Text Boxes** and positioned them above the **Smart Art**, rotating one item to call attention to it.

> **Plus:** Note how the template's conference logo is not so innocuous once you see it in slide after slide.

It took me more time to settle on a particular form of the **Smart Art** – lots of choices, not all of them useful – than to create the rest of the slide material.

Note that I could choose to put the timeline on a single slide. It is, after all, a single idea.

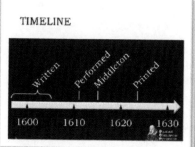

I like the slide on the left better. I think it's clearer… but it also took somewhat more work. (It wasn't hard, but it did take more time than than the one on the right.)

What's the difference between either version of this slide and the quartet on the facing page? In One Idea per Slide, it matters what the specific idea is.

On this page, the idea is the timeline: these events happened in the course of about twenty years, in a relatively logical sequence (even Middleton's rewrite was semi-logical, as he and the King's Men, Shakespeare's theater company, tried to keep the play "fresh" so audiences would continue to return… with coin in hand).

The opposite page focuses on specific aspects of the play's history – its creation, the time between writing and first recorded performance, and so on.

It's not that one approach is better than the other, in a vacuum. We do not present in a vacuum (where it would sure be hard to speak). What is the *context* in which the slide lives?

Time, thou anticpatest my dread exploits.
William Shakespeare, *Macbeth*

Example: Information Session List

Smart Art lets me introduce graphical elements even into what is primarily an all-text presentation (p. 100), without requiring either a bunch of hard work or a high level of artistic competence.

Consider the last point on the slide on p. 59, the sources of the text in this conference lecture. It's a list of alternatives.

I could have used bullet lists, but they look ordinary at best. Instead, I created the version on the opposite page. (Total time, less than two minutes for the core slide, another minute to pop in the little bullet-pictures of Shakespeare.)

It took only a minute to find a useful piece of **Smart Art**. As with the four timeline slides in the preceding spread, I gave it a 3D look using the same **Metallic Scene** button. I did take that extra minute to add pictures of Shakespeare as "bullets." I don't know that the slide needs these, really, but it's an example of what's possible with just a little extra work.

(My personal style would likely use these bullets because I can get the audience to laugh about them. However, humor can be dangerous ground for a presenter. If you have confidence in your ability to elicit laughter at the proper moments, go for it; nothing livens up a presentation more, especially at a conference where attendees have likely been sitting through nothing but painful Death by PowerPoint experiences. However, if you have any doubts about using humor, don't. If you feel awkward or tentative about it, the audience will know and become uncomfortable themselves.)

Plus: Dropping one Smart Art into an all-text presentation can be jarring. Find your visual style (p. 96).

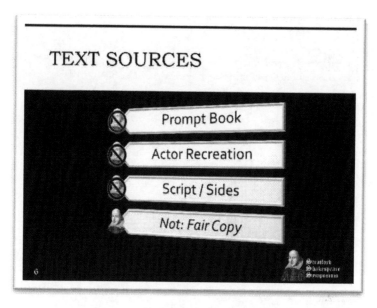

Animating or "Building" Lists

PowerPoint makes it easy to have list elements appear one at a time, as you work the clicker. Go to the **Animations** menu and click the **Appear** (or **Fade**) button. Under **Effect Options** on that menu bar, select **By Paragraph** (for text) or **One by One** (for **Smart Art**).

However, I usually avoid these "builds" for bullet points/lists. The onscreen movement causes attention to snap back to the slide just as I start talking about a new point – the exact opposite of where I want the audience to focus. I'm not single-minded about these builds, and I actually do use them from time to time when a) I have the slide displayed for a longish time as I introduce each new element or b) when I have a legitimate reason for not wanting the audience to "read ahead," say because one of the elements in the list is unexpected.

So come, fate, into the list!
William Shakespeare, *Macbeth*

Refining the Information Session Example

The slides on the preceding spread are probably fine as is. I'd suggest spending more time practicing your talk than dinking further with the slides.

Still....

The key point on each of the first four slides isn't necessarily as clear as it could possibly be. If I

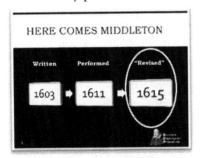

wanted to spend a bit more time, I'd draw a circle around the key items (the middle date on the Written slide, the final date on the other three), like the slide at left. I'd use a bright red "circle" to contrast with the black-and-white style of the presentation.

With a touchscreen laptop, I'd manually draw the circle "live," in front of the audience. This manipulation takes some practice, but it really makes the audience feel part of the presentation, and helps get across the idea that you're working hard to give them your best effort. It also, of course, calls extra attention to the key item – at the *right* time!

Lacking a touchscreen, use the **Drawing/Oval** tool to lay down an oval. Use **Drawing/Shape Fill** to say **No Fill**, leaving only the border of the circle and letting you see through it to the text below.

Plus: You don't *have* to refine one-idea slides. Simple is effective. See the chapter on Visual Styles (p. 95).

Then use **Drawing/Shape Outline→Weight** to make the line thicker, and **Drawing/Shape Outline→Color** to change the color.

Finally, grab the "**handles**" of the shape – the small circles at each corner and side – to adjust the circle to your desired size.

All that sounds harder than it actually is. Once you've drawn half a dozen circles, these steps will come automatically.

Also, once you're created one you like, simply **Select** it from its slide, **Copy** it, and **Paste** it into the new slide. I usually create from scratch only one of these highlighting circles in a given presentation. Once I build one in the presentation's style and color, I copy/paste it to other slides that call for a circle-highlight.

Animate the Circle?

Want to make the circle "draw itself"? Select **Animation/Wheel**, and it will look like you're drawing it even without a touchscreen. You may want to adjust the **Timing/Duration** to half or three-quarters of a second. Animations also come along for the ride with copy/paste, so once you get one circle working, you can simply replicate it, resizing it as needed on subsequent slides.

I like the dynamics of these particular animations (e.g., circling key items) because it fits my presentation style, but they're not for everyone. If it doesn't fit your style, or if it feels like one more thing to worry about during the actual presentation, don't do it.

And for sure, don't get carried away with animations. Use them to replicate what you might do at a white board, say.

Or Think Graphically

A timeline is a natural graphic element. Consider **Smart Art** or other graphics that clarify timelines.

The wheel is come full circle.
William Shakespeare, *King Lear*

Presenting Your Content

Your modified presentations may seem "longer" because they have many more slides. Don't let that throw you. (You may need to explain to conference organizers that your slides go by quickly, lest they envision a fifty-slide deck lasting four hours rather than forty-five minutes.)

This format also requires you to be comfortable advancing slides, either from your laptop or – better – with a remote "clicker" or slide advancer (p. 171). When you get to your presentation site, take some time if possible to practice with the clicker, especially if it's not yours but belongs to the presenting organization. One Idea per Slide does call on you to keep the slides moving along.

You can also choose on the fly how much time you'll devote to each slide/idea, since your slide is no longer filled with text that cries out to be covered. As in the conference session example on p. 60, you control the level of detail based on the audience's need, the available time, and the rhythm of the presentation.

For example, if you're looking for audience interaction and not getting much, it's easy, with few words on a slide, to ask, "What do you think this means?" Or, "Who agrees with this? Raise your hands."

Or perhaps you realize you've been rushing. You could use a small digression, tell a brief but relevant story, or dig deep into your notes. "1603. Elizabeth dies, and James takes the throne – not without controversy. How did this affect Shakespeare and the writing of *Macbeth*?" (Willie stuck in a dream sequence showing James as one of Banquo's descendants.)

Plus: One Idea per Slide offers you far more control over your presentation than word-filled slides.

Running Out of Time

You should have a good idea of how long your presentation will take because you've practiced it. Aloud. More than once. However, sessions start late. Questions and discussion take up time (and those are good things, because the audience is engaged.) You miscalculate. You get caught up in an unplanned digression because it fits for that particular audience. For whatever reason, you realized you have five minutes left and five content-rich slides you haven't yet gotten to.

You have four choices.

- Apologize to the audience. "Sorry we couldn't get to everything." I'm not a fan of this choice.
- Rush through the slides, speaking quickly. Nah. Not good.
- Hit only one high-level point on each slide and move on to the next. The One Idea per Slide format makes this approach perfectly reasonable because you *don't* have a bunch of text that the audience knows you're skipping – and that they're trying to read as you rush to the next slide.
- Skip (branch, p. 162) to your closing slide, or to another chosen slide near the end. I try to arrange my presentations, especially those where I expect an interactive relationship with the audience, so that I can easily and fluidly omit material as I approach the end of a session. I would rather have a collaborative, attentive audience than worry about making every single point in my presentation.

The easiest slides to skip are summaries, wrap-ups, and opportunities for questions (assuming you've been taking questions as you present). I recommend preparing your presentations so that you can comfortably skip these slides – and then practicing the skips until you can do them smoothly and without the audience aware of it (unless they compare their handouts).

With a dropping industry they skip.
William Shakespeare, *Pericles*

Exceptions to One Idea per Slide

There are a few types of slides that don't fit a literal One Idea per Slide approach. Let's summarize some exceptions here, along with suggestions on how to handle them to avoid Death by PowerPoint.

Note, however, that at a high level these all retain One Idea per Slide. It's just that the slide is then filled with details, sub-ideas, etc. that you can't easily or logically extract into individual slides.

Deep Data Dives

Sometimes you need to present – usually for group discussion – significant quantities of data, such as a budget issue, scientific results, etc. Supply copies of the data to the attendees if possible, so they can follow along on paper rather than squinting at the slide. (If they're not going to be looking at you, at least let them focus on something easily readable – and *your* content rather than email.)

You can use the projected version to circle/highlight specific numbers or areas of the data to explain or discuss. Use the data's native form. Don't try to convert it to bullet points.

Extracts From a Document

If you're presenting a passage for discussion – or even multiple compare-and-contrast extracts – you have little choice but to put them on screen. Don't read them aloud. Do give the audience time to read them – and tell them you're giving them time.

Plus: The perfect is the enemy of the good. If you absolutely can't limit a slide to one idea, don't.

Parallel Text (e.g., Survey Responses)

Sometimes you have to display a series of sentences, such as verbatim responses to a survey (as per my example on p. 130). Classic bullet points. Not a whole lot of options here... but if possible, provide handouts as well, again for ease of reading. Look over my real-life story on that spread (p. 130) for ideas on how to avoid the let's-all-read-the-slide problem.

Long Lists

Lengthy lists are occasionally unavoidable – steps in a scientific procedure, potential topics for discussion, stakeholders on a project – where you need the audience to be aware of the list but you don't need to discuss every item separately.

For loads of short items, use two columns to ensure the type doesn't grow too small, via the standard PowerPoint **layout** called **Two Content** (p. 156). Grab the **handles** on the two-column text boxes and expand the boxes to take up as much screen real estate as possible. It text is still too small, consider dispensing with the title box, or use **Paragraph/ Line Spacing Options** to **Remove Spacing Before** each paragraph and/or set **Line Spacing** to **Multiple** at **0.9** (meaning lines use only 90% of the standard line-height spacing).

Summaries, Agendas, etc.

Summaries and agendas are also lists of a sort. Try to limit them to no more than seven items (five is ideal) of one to three words each, so that the audience can pick them up at a glance (scan) rather than having to read them.

My lady takes great exceptions.
William Shakespeare, *Twelfth Night*

Five Takeaways

1. One slide, one idea. One Idea per Slide. Stronger slides, easier to create, simpler to speak to.

2. Leave supporting points off the slide when possible. Speak to them instead – or not, depending on time and flow when you give the presentation.

3. If supporting points require visibility – e.g., critical facts you need the audience to evaluate and/or retain, put them on their own slide(s).

4. Not every point must be made in onscreen words. Use **Presenter View** notes as reminders if you're worried you'll omit a critical bit of information.

5. There are exceptions to One Idea per Slide, but use them judiciously. Near-Death by PowerPoint isn't the kind of improvement you're looking for, or deserve.

Next Steps/Action Items

- Rework a few of your existing busiest slides in the One Idea per Slide format. Give a mock presentation (aloud or subvocalized "to yourself," but without an audience) so you can see how it works.

- Practice the draw-a-circle technique on p. 67.

- After you read the next chapter, circle back and think about how the slides you're creating fit the map described there.

Being the right idea.
William Shakespeare, *Richard III*

What's *THAT* to the PURPOSE?

3. EACH SLIDE HAS ONE PURPOSE.

DEFINE. ENHANCE. SHOW DATA. SIGNPOST. BUT NEVER ECHO.

Good slides not only have a single idea, but also a clear purpose. Most "Death-by" slides echo what the speaker is saying… which is the one purpose you should generally avoid.

What's the Point of This Slide?

Each slide in a presentation should have a purpose that supports your goal for the presentation as a whole.

Seems straightforward, right?

Project Description

▶ Source candidates from a larger pool
▶ User population
    ▶ 38 external recruiters
        ▶ "Headhunters"
    ▶ 21 internal recruiters
    ▶ 346 HR generalists and specialists
    ▶ Hiring managers worldwide
▶ 4500 hires annually
▶ Project delivery: 14 months

So what's the purpose of the slide at left, from Bad Example #1 (p. 30)? The title tells you something about the content, but what's the *purpose*? Why is it in the deck? Why is it the first content slide after the title? What is the speaker hoping to achieve with respect to the audience?

You could say that this slide started with a single *idea*, but it lacks a clear *purpose*.

Describing the project is not a purpose. Helping the audience understand why the project is important *might* be a purpose, but the slide speaks to that point only on some of the bullets – and in a business shorthand that makes sense to the HR team but not necessarily to the audience, representatives of the CFO and CIO who control funding.

> **Plus:** You don't *have to* think about the purpose of each slide, but doing so increases your effectiveness.

Five Purposes: Four Good, One Not So Good

A slide can have one of five purposes, each described in detail in the five following spreads. Four of these purposes generally add value to your presentation, and to the audience. The fifth is usually less successful.

Define the Concept: Introduce or explain a concept to the audience. Use these slides when you define a concept, abstract an idea, or in general give the audience a new way to think about something.

Enhance the Concept: In effect, these slides represent the old bullet points. Of course, by now you have better ways to present the material than a bunch of bullet points.

Show Data: Sometimes you need to share significant amounts of data. These information-rich slides usually leave the audience focused on the screen and/or their handouts. There is a time in many presentations where this is necessary and desirable – e.g., discussing a budget, reviewing an experiment, ranking alternatives.

Note that the slide on the opposite page combines these first three purposes into a mishmash that confuses rather than enlightens the audience – and removes the focus both from the presenter and from the goal the presenter is trying to achieve.

Signpost the Concept or the Presentation: These slides help the audience get their bearings within a presentation (an agenda, say) or navigate a complex idea.

Echo the Speaker: This is the traditional bullet-point-laden slide that kills presentations, although there are some effective ways – and times – to echo the speaker to emphasize a point.

Ay, there's the point.
William Shakespeare, *Othello*

Slides That Define a Concept

In One Idea per Slide, the purpose of certain slides is to define a concept. (Most enhance it, covered in the next spread.) Note that the projected content alone needn't carry the definition. Rather, the "slide" represents the combination of what you as presenter say plus the words and/or images on the slide.

In a short presentation, devoted to exploring a single concept, the title slide might be the only "define" slide. The title of the seminar in Bad Example #2 (p. 32), "Transcription Errors in the First Folio's *The Tragedy of Macbeth*," makes very clear (to the intended audience, at least) the concept at stake.

On the other hand, the title of Bad Example #1, p. 30, "IT Budget Meeting," offers little guidance. The subtitle, "Project Reindeer Funding Request," isn't a whole lot better unless for some reason the project's name is well-known.

Standalone presentations generally need a slide that defines the purpose of the presentation, if for no other reason than to mark the transition from before-presentation to in-presentation. A brief presentation within the context of a meeting – "Susan's going to detail problems on this project" – might be fine without one.

Each section of a longer presentation may form a concept needing definition. For example, a presentation on time management might have sections on email, low-value tasks, to-do lists, working with difficult people, and so on. Each should be introduced with a slide that defines the concept. You're not trying to define email itself, of course, but rather alert the audience that you're going to discuss ways to be more productive with regard to email.

Plus: Use definitional slides sparingly – and definitions that echo your words even more sparingly.

The presentation would likely also have a slide defining the concept of time management itself.

The IT budget example of the previous spread almost certainly needs a slide defining Project Reindeer – followed by slides that explain (enhance) the concept.

Defining Terms

Terms often require definition slides as well.

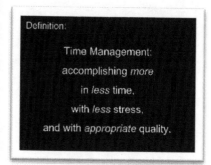

For example, the time-management presentation might define time management as, "Accomplishing more in less time, with less stress, and with appropriate quality." Because this definition lays out not just the obvious, captured in the first phrase in this example, but the presenter's emphasis, it's worth committing to words on a slide.

For simple definitions, you can choose to project the term and give the definition yourself, which puts the emphasis on you as the source of information, or you can echo the wording on screen, which puts the emphasis on the words themselves.

I recommend echoing definitions that require more than a single phrase and that are important to your presentation – e.g., I'd echo onscreen the definition of time management in this example, but I'd probably avoid an onscreen definition of multitasking because an exact definition doesn't really help get the message across to the audience.

Define a little touch.
William Shakespeare, *Henry V*

Slides That Enhance a Concept

Most of the slides in a presentation enhance rather than define concepts. The traditional bullet-point style mushes these together, minimizing the number of slides (which rarely matters) but defocusing the audience. Define your concept, and then provide a series of slides that enhance it, One Idea per Slide.

Fixing Bad Example #1

On p. 76 I showed a "project definition" slide from Bad Example #1 that that tried to do far too much. As a result, it confused rather than guided the audience. Let's start fixing the content. (We're not going to worry about the layout or design here. Those could use some help as well, but some very simple reworking of the concept will get us 80% of the way there with 10% of the work.)

Here are the first three slides of that fix, reserving the facts-and-figures portion for the next spread:

The first slide defines the concept, per the preceding spread.

Plus: "Enhance" slides form the meat of most presentations (except those that are dense with data).

Note the middle slide. The fictional company here, Amalgamated Ruminants, is not in the search business. They neither make a mail product nor offer a button to "friend" people. The decision-makers in the room know that. They're probably looking askance at the presenter... who sure has their attention.

"We compete with them to hire the best candidates. The people who can take our business to a new level." Now they're interested.

(By the way, were I building these slides for a real company, I might check if I could include the relevant logos under Fair Use laws, though the simple starkness of these slides also has power.)

The third slide explains further. These slides enhance the concept that Project Reindeer will help the company. But rather than jamming them together as so many presenters do, you can give each idea room to shine, without competition from the other ideas around it, however related they may be. Trust the audience to remember what you said sixty seconds ago.

Note how simple the text is on each of these slides. One idea. Easy to grasp, easy to speak to. And large enough to read (48 pt.) from the back of the room, without glasses. (Also observe the period at the end of each sentence. It's a subtle effect, but it makes a difference in how readers see the sentence. Note how many ads use periods as well – and you know they're testing every possible variant to see which is the strongest at inducing action!)

Note also that I have not repeated the Project Reindeer title. It's unnecessary, takes focus from the main idea, and dilutes the simplicity of the slide. The name is definition. These slides are enhancers.

Of course, the text of these slides isn't to be found on the original, but the ideas were lurking underneath. *Someone* in HR wants this project to bring in better candidates. Don't lose the most important element of the presentation!

Herein mean I to enrich.
William Shakespeare, *A Midsummer Night's Dream*

Slides That Show Data

"One Idea per Slide" and "no bullet points" doesn't mean you'll never have slides filled densely with material. Rather, you reserve that style of slide for appropriate times.

Some types of presentations involve significant amounts of data. Budget discussions. Scientific reports. Sales projections. Survey results. All rely on quantities of data.

Not all of the data is tabular, either, suitable for a spreadsheet (or other tabular layout). Look back at the original Project Reindeer slide on p. 76, for example. It contains some facts and figures regarding the user population for this proposed software system. The numbers are interesting for the target audience. They're also meaningful, such that the audience would benefit from seeing them rather than simply hearing from the speaker that the project will have hundreds of users. Thus it's worthwhile incorporating them into a slide, such as this revised version (which is all text, other than the horizontal line, and thus extremely simple to create).

By the way, note that the original referred to "headhunters" and revealed that two classes of HR folks would use the system. However, slide text is shorthand; keep it simple. The presenter can mention that HR includes both specialists and generalists – and that maybe there are contract workers as well as employees. That information isn't germane to the core idea of the slide: improving this system will help lots of users. (I did retain "worldwide," because global applicability is likely a major selling point.)

Plus: Ensure spreadsheet data is readable, either by enlarging it on screen or giving the audience copies.

Incorporating Spreadsheets

I'm not a fan of copying spreadsheets into a presentation. I'd rather display the actual spreadsheet program on the screen while the audience examines their own copies, on paper or their laptops (for budget discussions, say, where the decision makers will likely want to try alternate versions of your numbers).

Sometimes it makes sense to copy a static image of the spreadsheet in order to flag certain areas with circles (p. 67) or other presentation-program-based highlight options (such as enlarging a section and overlaying it on the original).

Graphs and Charts

Charts and graphs, on the other hand, are often better displayed in PowerPoint, where you have greater control over the way they look. Once confident the numbers won't change, create the chart or graph in whatever tool you prefer – e.g., Excel™ – and then paste it *as an image* into PowerPoint (**Paste**, then **Ctrl**, then **u**).

One option is to keep modifying the original – labels, text size, etc. – until you like the result. However, in many programs, making these changes requires both knowledge and good mouse control to click specific pixels. The latter is not easy if you're assembling the presentation on a plane, say. The other option is to enlarge the graph to the size you want within PowerPoint, crop out all of the text, and then add large text annotations judiciously.

You could link the PowerPoint image back to, say, the Excel original, so that when you change the spreadsheet, the PowerPoint image reflects those changes. However, the time and knowledge required to make this work suggest that for most of us, it's easier to simply display the Excel version, forgoing the improved visual quality to spend time on other areas.

I'll wipe away all trivial fond records.
William Shakespeare, *Hamlet*

Slides That Signpost

Both complex (multi-concept) presentations and complex ideas should offer signposts to help the audience navigate. Signposts take the form of either street signs or itineraries.

Street Signs

A street sign tells you where you are, period – e.g., the corner of Elm and Main. It presumes you will supply the context, such as the name of the town. A scientific report, for example, doesn't need context; the sections are always the same, usually in a specific order as well.

Here's a street sign for the presentation on time management discussed on p. 79. It tells the audience that we're going to seek a specific definition for what can be a nebulous concept. Indeed, in giving this presentation I sometimes ask the audience for their own definitions as a way of learning what's on their mind. (I'm not

probing for specific definitions as much as the particular issues that concern them – so I can make sure I touch on them later.)

Street signs within a presentation need not be echoed on slides. For example, in my long-form seminars I take a moment, about fifteen minutes in, for "housekeeping" – a discussion of breaks, locating the rest rooms, and so on. No slide says "housekeeping" (except that *I* know which slide triggers my covering these points), but it's a signpost, "you are here" moment nonetheless.

Plus: Signposts help the audience orient themselves when you move between topics.

Itineraries

Itineraries provide both location and context – e.g., we're at the third topic in our five-item agenda.

Itineraries can serve two purposes. One, of course, is obvious – helping the audience understand where they are in the flow of a presentation, the third-topic-of-five item.

However, itineraries also allow you to recapitulate the concept of every section up to this point. For example, if I were teaching a class on the Bill of Rights, I'd probably divide it into ten sections, one per amendment. Each time I reach a signpost for the next amendment, I'd summarize the previous ones – or ask the class to call out the "street sign" versions of the ones covered so far. By the time I reached the tenth amendment, the class would likely remember the key concepts of each of first nine. (Given that most everyone already knows what the first and second amendments cover at least at a superficial level, and few know anything about amendments eight or nine, I'd probably structure this class as a countdown, starting with the tenth amendment. By the time we talk about freedom of speech, religion, and the press, someone will have called out, say, "unenumerated rights" enough times to remember the ninth amendment. Which brings up another point – the right order of concepts for your talk is the one that will encourage the audience to remember the information, or lean toward the action you're urging. Don't be afraid to rearrange your presentation once you've assembled the component parts.)

It's a personal preference as to whether to use a street sign or an itinerary to separate the sections of a unified presentation. Clearly, a group of disconnected topics calls for agendas/itineraries. However, if the topics all relate logically to a common theme, you decide on the form that makes sense. (My own preference is for street signs when possible, to cut down the word count.)

Thou has seen these signs.
William Shakespeare, *Antony and Cleopatra*

Slides That Echo

Recall that people cannot listen and read at the same time.

 Yet far too many slides echo the speaker's words, in a pseudo-shorthand that seems almost designed to create dissonance between our ears and our eyes, summed up by Peter Norvig's PowerPoint Gettysburg Address (norvig.com/Gettysburg/).

There are times for brief echoing, such as:
- Agendas and other itineraries (p. 85).
- Definitions (defining a concept often echoes it).
- Summaries of key lessons of the presentation (see below).
- Critical ideas (no more than a phrase – e.g., the touchstone for each amendment in the Bill of Rights).
- Title, subtitle, and author of a presentation.

For the most part, these slides where echoing is okay are signpost and definition slides.

Shorthand Echoes

I can think of few times where a presentation has been improved by extended echoes, where the slide repeats the speaker's words. Condensing those onscreen words into some sort of buzzword phraseology doesn't improve the result.

Yet this is what you see in presentation after presentation. The speaker has three or four or five points to make on a given subtopic. Each of those points is bulleted on the slide, usually in a sort of shorthand that omits critical parts of speech (like the subject, and often the verb as well).

Plus: Echoing your words on screen is deadly dull except for a handful of special cases.

You won't forget what you're going to say. You have your notes. You have One Idea per Slide, which ensures that your key ideas get served up to the audience. And you have your knowledge, your expertise, the reason the attendees are there in the first place.

Finally, if you're in effect reading your slides, the *audience* will forget what you had to say. It's much harder to process the content against the discordance of hearing one form of it while reading a similar-but-different form. Don't let your fears cause the audience to work double-hard... because most of them won't.

Summarizing Slides

One last type of useful echo is the summary slide at the end of the presentation, or of one of its sections. If you've made five important points in a twenty minutes talk, you may find it useful to reinforce those points for the audience.

These kinds of summaries do work – as long as the points you make are spelled out as briefly as possible, ideally with just a keyword or two. Going back the the Bill of Rights example (p. 85), the summary slide might look something like this – a particularly difficult example because the list, at ten items,

The Bill-of-Rights Countdown

10. State powers
9. Unenumerated
8. Bail, Punishment
7. Civil jury
6. Speedy trial

5. Due process
4. Search
3. Quartering
2. Arms
1. Press, Speech, Religion

is too long to be effectively read. Short of rewriting the Constitution, however, there's no way to reduce the number of items. All the presenter can do is strive to keep them short.

Bullet lists sure are ugly, though. Luckily, a "bullet list" isn't restricted to a column (or two, in this case) of PowerPoint bullets.

Speak the fool slides!
William Shakespeare, *Troilus and Cressida*

Better "Bullet" Lists

A "list" is a collection of items. Nothing says it has to be arranged vertically, or have some form of bullet character to set it off.

 This page features a dozen different variants of lists. All are available at SlideStrong.com/BulletLists with both light and dark backgrounds. These aren't necessarily the most elegant, best executed, etc. I've created them to spark your own imagination. If you're a zoologist, try pictures or outlines of animals. Aeronautics engineer? How about airplane shapes, or a coach-class seating diagram? Or explore the range of **Smart Art** (see also p. 152; slides on this spread *based on* **Smart Art** have a checkmark in the corner.)

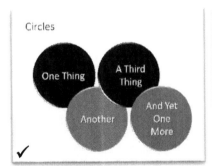

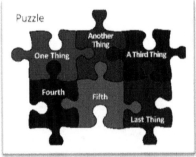

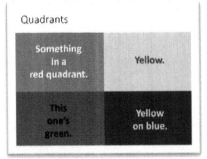

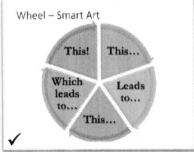

Plus: The only magic to bullet lists comes from getting away from the default list-of-bullets form.

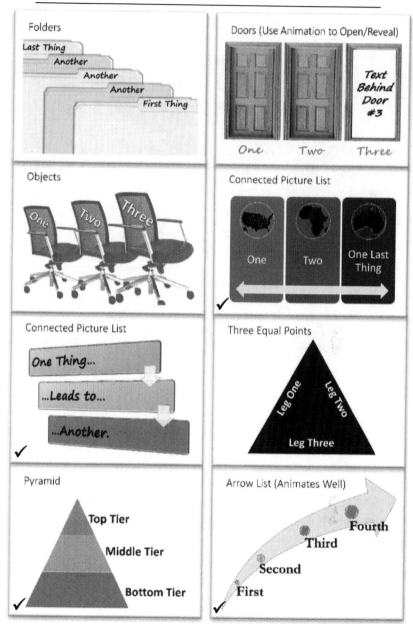

Be so bold or daring-hardy as to touch the lists.
William Shakespeare, *Richard II*

Five Takeaways

1. With slides that *define* a concept, use them sparingly, and keep them short.

2. Most of your presentation should (usually) be made up of slides that *enhance* your concepts. Be creative!

3. Use *signposts* to help the audience keep their place in a presentation, and to provide transitions between sections.

4. Reserve *echo* slides for itineraries, definitions, *brief* summaries, etc.

5. Don't echo your actual material, unless you want your slides to compete with you – a boring battle in which you and your slides both lose.

Next Steps/Action Items

- Go through some of your existing slide decks and categorize the purpose of each slide – define, enhance, show data, signpost, or echo. Note that some slides may serve more than one purpose – in particular, slides that define concepts may also legitimately echo the presenter's words.

- Single out a few "shorthand" echo slides, those with multiple bullet points that echo in condensed form what you planned to say. Revise them using One Idea per Slide, and give each a clear purpose.

- Try revising one or two of those shorthand echo slides to a single define-the-concept slide. In effect, save the title and throw out the body of the slide. Now practice speaking to that slide. Feel free to use the old content as slide notes if you have two monitors, or print it out and used it as handheld notes. It may feel awkward – or scary – the first time. Try it a few times until your voice becomes animated and you engage in imagined dialog or persuasion with your audience. (Dogs make good audiences to practice on. Cats may be less supportive.)

What's that to the purpose?
William Shakespeare, *Twelfth Night*

DETAILS,
DETAILS,
DETAILS

The first half of this book has talked about why fixing your slides is an important part – probably the most important/easily fixed part – of improving your presentations, and shown you three easy steps you can take.

The second half of this book contains additional details and related topics touched on in that first half. Visual styles, suggestions for specific types of presentations, tips on working with PowerPoint as you design your slides, steps you can take during the actual presentation, and more.

He hath CHANGED his STYLE.

YOUR VISUAL STYLE.

CREATING A PRESENTATION STYLE THAT WORKS FOR YOU.

The best presentations have a cohesive visual style – one that works for the presenter, for the specific presentation, and for the venue.

But as Emerson said, "Foolish consistency is the hobgoblin of little minds." Pick whatever works for you. Just <u>having</u> a style is 80% of the battle. Refine it later, but start doing something – anything! – besides the default bullet-point approach.

What's a Visual Style?

A visual style is the "look and feel" of your presentation slides. Are the slides light text on a dark background or dark text on a light background? Black and white or color? Which colors? Which fonts? Do you use graphics intensively, occasionally, or not at all? Lots of slides? Only a few slides? Whole sections with no slides at all, just a black screen?

There's no one right answer. There are only answers that are right for you. Most presenters mix and match (p. 108).

Some Examples

 Harvard Professor Lawrence Lessig is famous for slide decks with hundreds of slides, most of which contain only one or two words, or perhaps an image, and go by in a second or two. Check out his 2011 talk at Google (note: contains political content, but for purposes of this book, focus on the form rather than the politics). This style is very hard to replicate, since what you say must conform exactingly to the material on your slides, almost like lip-synching. However, even relatively inexperienced presenters can use brief excerpts of this style, such as flashing through the key words of a definition. Also, note how well it conforms to One Idea per Slide, sometimes One Idea Divided Into Many Slides (instead of the deadly normal, Many Ideas Crammed Into One Slide).

I know a terrific speaker whose all-text slides look like a bunch of words flung onto a screen without a moment's thought to formatting. I've come to suspect it's intentional, since it makes you look at *him* rather than the screen, but I'll omit his name just in case.

Plus: Use your smartphone to link to the QR codes. The links are also available on the book's website.

Garr Reynolds defines an approach called Presentation Zen, summed up in a beautiful short presentation by Matt Helmke (see the QR code at left). Look at how simple these slides are, how elegant in their simplicity. This presentation embodies One Idea per Slide.

At right is a QR code for a presentation Garr Reynolds himself gave at a Japanese TEDx conference. He uses a *lot* of slides for this particular talk – but they're all elegant and simple, never overstuffed, One Idea per Slide, in a flowing mix of images, words, or occasionally both. When he chooses to echo his words on screen (p. 86), it's for good purpose, usually quoting an Aikido (or Jedi) master. Note how he weaves the theme for his talk – bamboo – through each of the slides, sometimes as background, sometimes in the images. (Also check out the way he uses his eyes to get the audience to look at specific slides. "Never look at your slides" is another rule you can toss out the window.)

Speaking of TED, some TED presenters use very few slides, with large portions of the talk given in front of a blank screen, or in some venues a live picture of the presenter. In the talk (QR code at left) by Joshua Foer on memory, note that he uses specific graphics to illustrate points from time to time; otherwise, the screen behind him shows only his image. I'll talk more about this method in a bit (p. 106).

The Best Style

The best style is whatever works for you *and for your audience*. Some commonality among the slides is good, but it's not as important as ensuring the audience can focus on your key messages. Slides that look good are better than ugly slides, all things being equal – but ugly, simple slides that reinformce your message beat beautiful slides that compete with you.

I remember the style.
William Shakespeare, Love's Labor's Lost

Style: Visual Images

Not everyone learns best from words, whether heard or read.

Slides that use visual images – "graphics" – to impart their message can be extremely powerful on two fronts:

Information Processing: Studies show that associating images with ideas helps many people process and retain information better. In a spate of words – most from your mouth, plus more from your slides and/or handouts – at least an occasional image can help cement concepts and reinforce your ideas.

Emotional Impact: Think of the Twin Towers on fire or the napalmed girl running down the road. These particular images carry deep emotional power. (Close your eyes and visualize one of these pictures. What's happening to your heart rate?) Your presentation may not call for an image with this level of resonance. Indeed, an image of such power might work against you in many settings. However, there may be moments in your presentation that call for a deeper connection between you and the audience (or among audience members), wherein you might utilize a picture that carries emotional weight.

Use images to replace, reinforce, or modify the slide's message. Slides may offer text with the images – or not. Do what works.

Examples: Literal

Class Lecture on Gettysburg: Show pictures of the battlefield, both then and now. For people who haven't been there, the size of the field across which Pickett charged is mind-boggling.

Sales Call: Show the product in use, ROI (payback) graphs, etc.

> **Plus:** In image-based slides, the important words come from you. Don't limit yourself to literal pictures.

Conference Session (Bad Example #2, p. 32): When you talk about the First Folio, show the text-as-image from it.

Examples: Illustrative or Metaphorical

Time Management Training: Clocks. Lots of clocks, even in unexpected places (see the image on p. 84). Plus maps of daily rhythms, email inboxes, slot machines, and more (next spread).

Facing a Problem: The Titanic, of course, but for smaller problems, how about a rowboat or small powerboat hung up on a rock? Or an astronaut ("Houston, we have a problem")?

Difficult Customers: Do they have to be people? See the more-with-less hippo in the next spread.

Decisions: Balance scales. Doors. (Maybe a picture of Monty Hall, for an older audience.) Forks in the road. Street signs. Smart Car vs. a luxury car. Be creative, metaphorical rather than literal.

Theme-Based: Maybe each page of the time-management session shows a different time-telling device. Or consider the various forms of bamboo running through Garr Reynolds' presentation in the preceding spread.

Images Don't Work in All Presentations

Note that Bad Example #1 (p. 30), requesting funding for an IT project, like many internal business presentations, offers little opportunity for visual imagery. In fact, many such presentations are diminished by inappropriate "business" graphics, such as pictures of happy customers or *Mad Men*-era stick-figure people. If you did have a screenshot of the very awkward user interface of the software you want to replace, however, it would help drive home the message of your need to increase productivity.

The true and perfect image.
William Shakespeare, *Henry IV pt. 1*

Visual Examples: Time Management Course

Here are some ideas on how to use images in a variety of ways — as example, as topic support, and more, all from a two-hour course on time management for professionals. All were created entirely in PowerPoint from stock images (e.g., without Adobe Photoshop™).

Note that some are literal (e.g., the graphs), some are metaphorical (e.g., the deep water of "gets you promoted"), and some are illustrative (e.g., playing "D" to email). Almost all are in color, with contrast hard to reproduce in a black-and-white book.

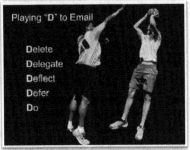 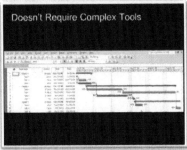

Plus: Some of these are more "elegant" than others. Doesn't matter. They illustrate points. They're not art.

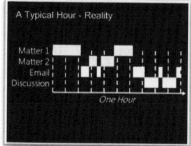

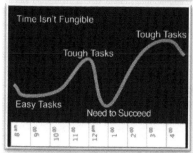

A friend of mine, the image.
William Shakespeare, *King John*

Style: Text Only

Text in brief bursts is powerful. We need to read; text compels us.

That's both a strength and a weakness. It's a weakness, of course, when it commands our attention at a time when we should be focusing on the speaker. However, brief bursts of text, even unadorned text, can help us pick up the key message of a slide or a presentation moment.

Larry Lessig (above) offers a powerful example. As noted on p. 96, few of us can replicate his style even if we wanted to, but we can learn from it. Finding ways to encapsulate moments in brief phrases, writ large upon a bright screen, can help drive home your message.

Font and Size

Text must be large and readable. For text-only slides, 48 points is a reasonable size. (For text mixed with images, 36 points works better.)

Font choice is personal for many presenters. If you don't want to worry about fonts, PowerPoint's default Arial or Calibri sans serif fonts work well enough.

If you prefer serif fonts, consider Garamond or Century.

(Font and layout experts will disagree, noting these are overused. They're right about that... but clichés become clichés for a reason. These fonts work for non-experts. That said, if you are comfortable with fonts and typefaces, absolutely explore beyond these quotidian choices.)

Plus: Remember, "text-only" still means One Idea per Slide – a few words, not multiple bullet points.

Arial:	The quick brown fox jumps over the lazy dog.
Calibri:	The quick brown fox jumps over the lazy dog.
Garamond:	The quick brown fox jumps over the lazy dog.
Century:	The quick brown fox jumps over the lazy...

Note the differences in apparent size (these are all set in 10.5-point type in the example above) – and in the amount of space the characters take up. Century and Arial, for example, spread out the text far more than Calibri or Garamond, which also have smaller "x-heights," the height of a lower-case letter.

Beware italics with serif fonts. *As you can see here with Garamond, many serif-font italics are compressed and hard to read beyond a word or two.*

Display Fonts

Display fonts – that is, fonts with more "style" or pizazz than my examples above – are useful for emphasis, such as the hippo's cry on the preceding spread.

However, most of these are hard to read and are thus ill-suited for the bulk of your content. There are a few easy-to-read display-style fonts not included with PowerPoint; you need to find and download them separately, which has its own difficulties. Don't choose blindly. If in doubt, stick with the standards, whether overused or not. Your job is to communicate, not win a design contest judged by criteria unrelated to the purpose of your presentation.

I often use handwriting-like fonts with animation to simulate writing on a slide. For example, on a slide showing "The Technical Problem," I "cross out" the word *Technical* (using animated lines, or drawing on my touch screen) and "write" the word *Business.* Since my handwriting is abysmal at best, and totally illegible when I try to write on a screen while talking, I use the very readable Segoe Print to simulate my onscreen emendation.

They have writ the style.
William Shakespeare, *Much Ado About Nothing*

Style: Diagrams and Maps

We use maps to find our way over unfamiliar terrain. (Or at least we used to. Nowadays, we listen to our GPS… and drive off the road, blindly following instructions from yesterday's geography.)

How can you use maps to help your audience find their way into your content?

Keep in mind that maps need not be literal representations of real (or metaphorical) terrain. The fabled map of the London Underground, all crisp angles and straight lines, doesn't reflect GPS truth but nonetheless effectively guides both visitors and locals. Any itinerary (p. 85) in your deck, such as an agenda, is also a map.

Note, for example, the two diagrams in the Time Management slides on p. 101. One maps the way a worker divides her time among four projects within an hour, another the level of energy and focus of this non-morning-person as the day wears on. Both illustrate points that wouldn't be nearly as clear in words alone.

Both also require the speaker's words in addition to the diagram. Don't clutter your maps with extraneous information. (If you want to provide instructions for use beyond the presentation, such as conference notes, employ handouts as suggested on p. 164.)

Examples

Timelines may be the most commonly used business diagrams, with a number of samples shown on p. 62. The two time-management maps noted above are both timelines.

Plus: Creating elegant or "artistic" maps is hard… and rarely worth the work. Shoot for *effective* instead.

Flowcharts are another common form of mapping, showing how one thing leads to another. That "thing" can be the work on a task, responsibility for that task, data, motivation, history, money, or almost any concept or tangible item with predecessors and successors. Avoid using standard flowchart symbols, however, unless your audience is already familiar with their meanings. For most people, arrows work just fine, as does one-item-piled-upon-its-predecessor.

Cause-and-effect ("fishbone" or Ishikawa) diagrams can be very powerful... but hard to read on screen. I've used them in project review presentations, but usually as handouts. (The onscreen version served as a placeholder – "now let's examine *this* element.") However, if you have but a handful of causes, you can make an onscreen-only fishbone diagram work – and it's an unforgettable image useful for driving home the point that most failures stem from multiple, semi-related causes.

Excel or charting-software charts are useful, but usually require additional formatting to make them readable on screen (discussed in more depth on p. 83).

Pie charts in particular let you show how a fixed quantity is divided – hours in a day, work allotted to team members, budget to departments, etc. As with other Excel-type charts, create the labels separately in PowerPoint to keep them readable.

Lists can be a type of diagram. Consider how many of the non-bullet list forms on p. 150 are also diagrams. At right is a **Smart Art** list/diagram describing leadership styles as defined in a landmark *Harvard Business Review* study by Daniel Goleman.

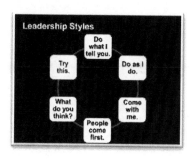

See this in the map.
William Shakespeare, *Coriolanus*

Style: Occasional Slides Only

The most valuable and overlooked PowerPoint feature is the **B** key while you're presenting. It blacks out the screen until you press it again.

(The **W** key "whites out" the screen, in case you want to make shadow pictures with your fingers or if the room lights fail.)

There are four places the **B** key can be effective in a presentation:

- If you are presenting in one section of a business meeting, you can have your slides ready to go but keep the screen blank to avoid the first slide being a distraction.
- When you stop to take questions, assuming you don't have a separate Questions slide.
- During breaks, especially a lunch break in a day-long class, though you can also use a signpost slide announcing lunch or the break.
- When you want to speak without anything on screen to pull the audience's focus.

The last is a powerful presentation technique.

Speaking Without Slides (for a Time)

Like most speakers, I sometimes tell stories to illustrate a point. Often I have a slide to illustrate the story, such as the checklist Captain Sullenberger used on the USAir flight that ended in the Hudson River. But sometimes the stories come in response to a question, or I can't find a slide that enhances a planned story.

> **Plus:** The no-slide option is scary, even for sixty seconds. But it's worth trying and can be liberating.

I want the audience to look at me, and I want to look in their eyes at these times, without the distraction of a slide. So I black out the screen. (My clicker, like most good clickers, has a button dedicated to this purpose.)

You don't have to limit the no-slide moments to storytelling. Perhaps you're offering an emotional plea for action. Or you're reaching the close of your sales presentation or budget request and want to talk directly to the decision maker, without giving her something else to look at. Or you simply can find nothing to put on the screen that adds value to the pont you're making.

In those cases, black out the screen.

Speaking With Just a Few Slides

You can also choose to speak with minimal slides. Maybe you have only one or two points you wish to make graphically, a style that many teachers uses. (Many TED talks use it as well.) Rather than leave a "stale" slide on screen, use the **B** key.

"Bursts" of Slides

Another option is to veer between bursts of slides and a black screen.

For example, you might choose to highlight or reinforce only definitions, which often come in bunches, and key concepts. You can build a powerful presentation presence in this way. Eyes will go to the screen only at specific times, under your control. The rest of the time, you have the chance to fully capture the audience's attention without the brightly lit distraction of a projected image or text.

Embrace the occasion.
William Shakespeare, *The Merchant of Venice*

Styles: Mixing and Matching

Most experienced presenters mix and match styles as appropriate for each section of their presentation.

(I recognize that many internal business presentations have strict formatting requirements – not just the design of the slides, but what goes on each slide. However, many of these are really discussions about handouts, where the screen ensures that people entering the meeting – or zoning out – know what page is under discussion. Let's omit these from discussion of styles.)

Generally, start building decks from the slide titles. (See the comments about **Outline View** on the facing page.) Don't spend time trying to define the content for each slide. Rather, capture the main idea, the One Idea per Slide.

Once you have a presentation that not only hangs together but appears to flow from point to point, then it's time to consider the right form for each of those points. Text only? A definition? A question? Maybe an image... but with or without a title? If you need a list, consider list alternatives (p. 150) – but don't get hung up in early stages trying to find the right choice. It's okay to leave lists as bullet items in the first pass through a deck. Fix them before the deck gets anywhere near presentation-ready, but don't get bogged down in details while you're still trying to understand the right flow for the content, ensure you have but One Idea per Slide, and perhaps build up your storyline (p. 187).

And remember, there is no "right" answer. Once you avoid the "wrong" answer – slides stuffed with details – you're on the way to better slides, and thus better presentations.

Plus: Be like the sculptor who finds magic by carving away everything that doesn't add value.

Transitioning From Bullet Points

The easiest way to move from Death by PowerPoint to One Idea per Slide is to start with a text-only deck.

For an existing deck, outline each of the points you want to make. PowerPoint has a serviceable **Outline View** (on the **View** menu). Give each idea, even each sub-idea, its own slide by making it a top-level outline entry – whether you modify your existing deck or keep it open for reference while you rework it into simpler form.

Then return to **Normal View**. Put a one- or two-word topic header in the **Title** box and distill your idea for that slide to no more than half a dozen words, focusing on One Idea per Slide and looking at the purpose of each slide (p. 76). No bullets. No sub-bullets or indented explanations or anything else. Just half a dozen words plus a title. (The title is optional. You may not need titles. If you use them, one title can span multiple idea slides.)

You can create a new presentation the same way, by starting with an outline. However, I recommend you at least glance at The Five Steps approach to better presentations summarized in the chapter starting on p. 187. Presentations based around a spine and a story are usually stronger than the "brain dumps" that outlining can sometimes engender.

Once you have a solid core, look for places where you might want to add visual content, whether images, maps, etc. Practice giving your presentation aloud (in private, or to a pet who won't judge you – dogs are good at this). See what works, what flows, what doesn't make sense – and readjust your slides to match.

As a final step, add a title slide and any necessary signposts (p. 84).

You may not yet have your best work, but you'll almost certainly have a richer deck that supports a stronger presentation, one that no longer delivers Death by PowerPoint.

He changed almost into another man.
William Shakespeare, *All's Well That Ends Well*

Light vs. Dark Backgrounds

We read dark letters on a light background, usually black on white. Our computers' screens today offer by default dark letters on light backgrounds, again usually black on white, as do e-readers and smartphones.

Even the default PowerPoint setting is black lettering on a white background.

Of course, the default PowerPoint layout is bullet points. Maybe we need to rethink this dark-on-light thing.

Various scientific studies over the past forty-plus years have proven... not much at all. For each study that supports dark-on-light, there is one that prefers light-on-dark. All I can do is offer some pros and cons.

In Favor of a Light Text/Dark Background

- Very effective in relatively dark rooms. Less strain on the light receptors (rods and cones) of both young and old viewers.

Light Text
on a
Dark Background

- Sets your work off from most run-of-the-mill presentations.
- Easier to achieve a professional look with less work.
- No glare from the screen (very noticeable in a dark room).
- Puts more of the visual focus on you, the speaker. Doesn't pull eyes to the screen as much as a bright background.

Plus: More important than dark vs. light: Text that is large, readable, and stands out against the background.

- Subtler change when you black out the screen (p. 106).
- Laser pointers show up better on dark backgrounds.
- Does not have an additional "frame" around the presentation. Most projection screens have a black border that frames dark-on-light slides but disappears into the background of light-on-dark slides.

In Favor of a Dark Text/Light Background

- More visible in brightly lit rooms.
- Much easier to format graphical images, especially using the **Remove Background** command. The majority of available "cutout" images are designed for white backgrounds.

> **Dark Text**
> **on a**
> **Light Background**

- Data and graphs usually show up better, but remember that detailed data is better left to the handouts.
- Handouts usually print out better, although as long as you stick to One Idea per Slide and larger type, you'll be fine either way.

About the Background

Generally, avoid pure white or pure black backgrounds. Consider, say, ivory instead of white, or a very deep blue or green (perhaps with bright yellow text) instead of black, either solid or with a barely visible texture and/or gradient.

For what it's worth, my own presentation preference usually features bright letters on a dark background, often yellow on a deep blue textured ground. I don't want a glaring, bright screen competing with me as a speaker. I will sometimes adapt to a client's color scheme... but only unwillingly to a supplied template (see p. 116 for more about such templates).

> *Dark shall be my light.*
> William Shakespeare, *Henry VI pt. 2*

Animations

There are three types of animations:
1. They reveal (or hide) elements, such as an item in a list.
2. Simulated writing/drawing on the screen.
3. Whizbang effects, such as moving stuff on the screen.

The first two can be valuable on occasion. The last... well, it can also be of use at times, but for the most part such animations are overused, intrusive, and not worth the effort they require.

Revealing List Elements

Revealing list elements is a common ploy with bullet points, but it works against you with items longer than a phrase. It directs the audience to focus on the screen at the very moment you need them listening to you because you're making a new point.

If in Doubt,

Many presenters have used list animations because they fear that when they reveal a new slide, audiences will spend too much time reading. Which is true... but the problem is the amount of text on the slide! With One Idea per Slide, this problem goes away.

With short list items, especially those in alternative "bullet-style" lists (p. 88), you may sometimes find value in animating the elements so that they reveal one at a time, especially if you plan to spend considerable time (e.g., thirty seconds or more) talking about each element. For example, when I teach people how to hold more productive meetings, I reveal each of the six elements separately as I address them for perhaps a minute apiece.

Plus: Animation guidelines: 1) Keep them unobtrusive.
2) They must add value. 3) Skip them if they're hard.

Writing on Your Slides

Writing (real or simulated) on your slides has been a powerful tool for teachers and others since… well, at least as long as overhead projectors and flip charts have been around.

With a stylus, a touchscreen, and a steady hand, you can write "live" on your screen – or simulate it with a "hand" font and the **Wipe** animation. (Apply it, choose **Effect Options**, then **From Left**.) See the ~~Technical~~ Business illustration on p. 103, for example. You may want to adjust the **Duration** slightly (in the **Timing** part of the **Animations** menu). Segoe Print is quite readable, or you can digitize your own handwriting.

Writing on your slide is a powerful way to say, "Not that, but this!" It's not a technical problem, but a business problem. We budgeted $1.1 million, but we brought the project home for $900K. Pickett wasn't the problem at Gettysburg; it was Lee's fault. (I'll hear from some Southerners about this one!)

Leave 'em Out!

Circling a key word or term is another form of writing on the slide. See p. 66 for a hint on how to make this animation work.

Moving-Object-Type Animations

Occasional broader animations can have their place, such as a door that reveals words behind it (a la Monty Hall – see p. 88). The guiding principle here is twofold: It shouldn't call attention to itself, and it should not require more work from you than the moment is worth.

And these animations do require work. If they're sloppy, you undercut whatever power you hoped they'd have.

No more moving.
William Shakespeare, *Othello*

Transitions, Prezi, etc.

Animations are visual effects *within* a slide; transitions are the effects *between* one slide and the next. They correspond to cuts or scene changes in a movie.

While crossfades and other effects used to be standard in films of, say, the 1940s, they're largely out of style. Remember the original *Batman* TV series? (If so, we're both showing our age!) It was heaped with goofy transition effects, which – intentionally – called attention to the artifice of the show. That's not what you're looking for when you present.

Tools such as Prezi are built around such whizzy transitions. Keynote pioneered many such effects (with PowerPoint later following suit), most of which were indeed cool, elegant… and intrusive.

Each time you consider a transition, ask yourself, How does it help me make my point? (Yes, Al Gore used some Keynote whizbang transition effects in *An Inconvenient Truth*, but he was offering a piece of theater with a message rather than presenting on a topic.)

Unless your topic is presentation software itself, or you're in the entertainment business, forget most transitions.

Transitions That Support Animations

Occasionally a presentation calls for a complex piece of animation that makes a topic clearer. For example, in teaching time management, I point out the danger of "urgent" interruptions.

> **Plus:** Transitions rarely add value. They add "coolth" – sometimes – but that's not the same thing.

Below is a sequence from this section, reproduced in loving black-and-white that doesn't capture the color elements very well (the publisher claimed printing in color would have made the book pricier for readers). When I present this material, I start by explaining the matrix, then introduce each element, highlighting the appropriate yes/no boxes on the border. The animations fade into each other because time is a continuum (and because it looks better in this complex sequence).

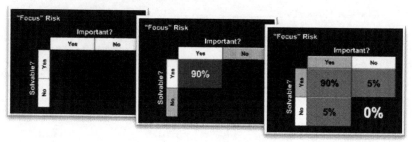

It's possible to animate this all on one slide, but it's a fair amount of work – and unnecessary. Instead, I spread this sequence across five slides – the introduction of the matrix, and then one for each element. Instead of fading in the various boxes and then dimming them, I used the **Fade** transition from one slide to the next. Thus I could get each slide correct on its own. Once I felt comfortable with the core look and feel of the matrix, it took little time to duplicate it and edit the individual slides.

In addition, I've reused this matrix structure in a number of presentations. (2x2 matrices can simplify – and admittedly over-simplify – many situations.) I no longer have to make difficult edits within a single slide when I reuse this sequence, where I would sometimes screw up the animation or ordering.

But... I'm not convinced this animation adds any value at all. I've been using this sequence for years, but that doesn't make it right. While I offer it as an example of how to use transitions in support of animations, I'll probably go back to a single, simpler slide.

Cut off the sequence.
William Shakespeare, *King John*

Organizational Templates

Inevitably, when you speak at a conference, or even in some business settings, the session organizer will email you a template and say, "Use this."

Run away.

If you can.

For starters, look at the two Bad Examples (pp. 30 and 32).

Note first how annoying the repeated organizational logo is on each page. (Bad Example #1 has the departmental motto too.) Bad Example #1 has a graphical element on each slide that adds no value – it's no better in color than it is in the black-and-white reproduction. Bad Example #2 forces the headings to all-caps, though at least it offers a font that's reasonably complementary to the subject matter of the conference.

Look, bad templates aren't the end of the world. They're not the biggest factor in the success or failure of your presentation.

But they rarely help you succeed.

Supplied Templates

If at all possible, dispense with supplied templates, except perhaps for the title slides. (Conference organizers and sponsors deserve that much.) You are being asked to present because of your subject matter knowledge. It is your material, not the template, that will make the session successful.

Plus: The more your reputation as a speaker grows, the easier these template battles become.

Conference organizers sometimes claim that they want to present a unified experience for the attendees. Given the vast range of topics, speaker skills and styles, and session formats, a template will do little by itself to create a unified feel.

It will simply make your presentation less effective unless your style and content happen to mesh with the template. How does that help create a better conference, or business meeting, etc.?

Obviously, this question may be sensitive for some organizers. It's certainly shouldn't turn into a major battle for you... but if you can negotiate your way out of the template, you're likely to get a better overall response from the audience (who will be seriously sick of the template by the end of the day).

Hiding the Template

Sometimes the easiest way to deal with the template is to accept it... and then hide it.

For example, suppose your preferred style uses a deep blue textured background. You can simply place that background as the **Send to Back** element individually on each of your slides after the title slide.

You may need to adjust the size, color, and font of the text on each templated slide as well. Given that most templates start out assuming you're going to squeeze a lot of bullet points onto each slide, you should get used to changing the fonts. Go into the Slide Master to make these changes (p. 156).

And bring your own copy of the presentation on a flash drive (thumb drive) if you aren't using your own laptop. You may need to substitute it for the version that got "re-template-ized." (Claim you made some last-minute updates.)

Who put my man in the stocks?
William Shakespeare, *King Lear*

Five Takeaways

1. Choose a visual style – image based, text only, heavy on maps and diagrams, or most often some combination of all of these.

2. Your style may vary with each presentation, or you may gravitate to a particular style that makes you most comfortable or gives you the most commanding presence.

3. Consider allowing portions of your presentation to proceed against a black screen (no slide).

4. Keep your animations simple, and ensure they add value in service of the idea of each given slide. Animations for animation's sake are bad ideas.

5. Transitions between slides are worse-than-useless most of the time, calling attention to your presentation skills rather than to the material you're presenting.

Next Steps/Action Items

- Watch clips of presentations on YouTube or other sources, starting with the clips referenced on p. 96.

- Experiment with brief presentations – three or four simple slides – in each of these styles, delivered aloud to, say, your dog. Or to no one. Just try them on for size.

- If you have a chance at work to deliver brief presentations in team meetings – again, a handful of slides, five minutes or so – try out some of these styles. Let the team know what you're doing, and get their feedback.

- If you think a given style might work for you, rework one of your previous presentations.

He hath changed his style.
William Shakespeare, *Henry VI, pt. 1*

what
have you NOW
to
PRESENT?

SPECIFIC PRESENTATION TYPES.

MORE THAN THE SAME OLD SAME OLD.

Even information-heavy presentations take more than standing at a lectern dispensing facts.

Sales Presentations

You're the product expert accompanying the sales team on a pitch to a potential customer. You'll demo the product, of course, but you also have to prepare some slides showing product features and future directions.

I licensed tens of millions of dollars of software and services in my corporate career, yet some of the most misguided presentations I've ever sat through accompanied these demos – quite a feat considering the presentation team supposedly included sales professionals. I've spent some time on the sales side of product and services presentations as well.

Start by putting yourself in the customer's shoes. What does she want to hear? What does she need in order to make two decisions: first, that your product can help, and second, that your product is the one she should champion.

If you can modify the presentation for each customer, ask the sales team about the key selling points *and objections* for the given customer. If it's a stock presentation, you can still get this information from the sales lead on the way into the room and adjust what you say on the fly. Even if you can't change the slides, One Idea per Slide gives you considerable flexibility to modify what you say in *response* to the slides.

Either way, are you responding to objections? Focusing on one or two benefits *specific to this customer*? Proving you're better at solving a particular problem than the incumbent or primary competitor? The same approach applies to the actual demo if you're pitching a product, by the way. (And don't get me started on bad demos. Someone needs to write a book on how to demo products, so I can force vendors to read it before they take up my team's time.)

Plus: Don't be afraid to ditch the slides and just talk – and listen. Communication wins customers.

Specific Suggestions

If you're selling a product, don't waste early time talking about yourself or your company. This information is valuable only after the customer has decided your product fits her needs.

Your first minute is the most important. Studies reveal that in personnel interviews, the interviewer makes up his mind within the first minute. A sales presentation is similar. What can you show in the first minute that will move the customer to your side? If you're not sure, at least don't show stuff they *don't* care about (see the preceding paragraph). Chances are that they have a problem they're trying to address. Explain how what you're offering solves that problem (with details to follow).

Let the customer talk. Indeed, encourage her to talk, to interrupt with questions. What you have to say and show is not nearly as important *to the customer* as answering her questions.

Figure out who in the room can say Yes. Most can only say No. (And many just talk without power to say either Yes or No.) Your lead sales professional should be the expert on this question, both from research and by picking up cues. If that's not you, develop a series of subtle signals such as knee-taps with him – respond to this person in detail, defer that question, etc. If you're filling both roles, keep the slides extra-simple so you can read the room rather than focus on your slides.

Use the customer's logo on your slides somewhere if you can.

Use branching (p. 156) to present slides "out of order" but seamlessly, whether in response to questions, shifting interests, reading the room, etc. Do not get stuck in a rote presentation.

The room is likely to be well lit, making the case for dark text on a light background (p. 111).

Sell when you can. You are not for all markets.
William Shakespeare, *As You Like It*

Fiscal (Budget) Reviews With Strict Templates

It's common in organizations for projects and/or departments to undergo periodic reviews of performance using a required format (template) that is almost entirely based on "the numbers."

You can't alter the template or format in this case... but you *can* (usually) do two things to make your presentation more effective:

1. Talk about the value you're bringing to customers, the company, the reviewing manager, etc. That's your core ("spine," p. 188) or your presentation, even if you can't reflect it literally in the preordained slides.

2. Highlight specific numbers in the slides visually.

Highlighting the Key Numbers

In PowerPoint: This is rarely an audience that wants – or will tolerate – bullet-point "builds" (animated entrances), moving numbers, or anything else that seems in the least flashy.

However, you can still highlight the items you want the audience to focus on using color (color the background of the text box, place a colored rectangle behind the number if the box is transparent, use the secret **Highlighter** tool, p. 148), or click the **Magnifier** icon that appears when you move the mouse during a presentation. Or circle the key numbers (p. 66).

Plus: No matter how constrained the format, you are still presenting. Take charge of your message.

If you have multiple numbers you want to highlight, each at a different time, you can use **Appear** and **Disappear Animation** to turn the highlights on or off. However, try the simple expedient of putting each group of highlighted numbers on an individual slide, duplicating the core data and then highlighting the specific numbers relevant for each slide, which allows you to jump to the right slide as the audience tosses out questions (p. 156).

In Excel: If you're presenting the numbers in a spreadsheet program, this step is technically more complicated and beyond the scope of this book. We often did present these in Excel when I ran departments and projects, but I would add a slide to the deck that highlighted the two or three numbers I wanted to focus on – circled, enlarged, colored differently, whatever best fit the message and the format.

Even when I presented these entirely in Excel, I would build a title tab (worksheet page) in Excel and create a "highlights" tab I could click on when I wanted to focus on my agenda or "story."

Non-Data-Oriented Slides

Keep your non-data slides simple, hewing to One Idea per Slide when possible. Consider the slides as reminders to the audience for the points *you* are making, rather than carrying the points themselves. The hard data belongs in handouts when possible, whether paper or electronic/online copies.

She cries, "Budget," and by that we know.
William Shakespeare, *The Merry Wives of Windsor*

Presenting Scientific Papers

Scientific reports follow one of a small number of standard formats – e.g., Title, Abstract, Introduction, Methods, Results, and Discussion. You have more flexibility with your presentation, even when you choose to deliver your talk using the same order as your research paper.

For one thing, you rarely need section titles on your slides, nor need you say, e.g., "I'd like to talk about our methods." Your listeners are familiar with this structure. And even when your abstract is a mini-summary of the other sections, you don't need to present it as such. Rather, state the problem you set out to address as crisply and dramatically as possible.

("Dramatically" applies to the context, of course. I don't necessarily mean "theatrically," but rather start with a simple and even slightly extreme version. Your audience is probably sitting through a large number of these papers, and traditionally only a handful of attendees are specialists in your field… and they've probably read your paper. So you can either take them aside for a discussion over sour conference-venue coffee… or find a way to make your work interesting to the room as a whole. It's exciting to you, right? Then share your enthusiasm!)

Methods

The audience isn't going to reproduce your work based solely on your slides. Unless you're figured out cold fusion, the details of your methods probably hold but minor interest to most attendees. Move quickly to the good stuff!

Plus: Give the audience a chance to absorb what you've worked so hard on. Don't crowd your slides.

Results

Had a breakthrough? Share it! Even if you haven't, you're adding to our collective knowledge store by your work... but only to the extent you share not just what happened but what it means vis-à-vis other work in your field. Anyone can read the paper. Use your time to put your work in context, especially for attendees who aren't experts in your particular slice of science.

Think about Dr. Feynman, the O-rings, and the glass of ice water (p. 43). Your audience is probably more scientifically sophisticated than his was that day. Nonetheless, amidst days of dry testimony, he found the way to make his point clearly and memorably. Remember that new insights come not only from your specialist peers but from others in related fields who see the world just a bit differently. This is your opportunity to engage them.

Discussion

Why not make it a real discussion? What do you want to know from the audience? What do you want to challenge them on? (Don't challenge individuals, of course. This isn't Science at the OK Corral.) I know that's hard. And it won't work in all venues. But you've got some incredibly bright minds in the room, and you have their attention, and surely all of you together are smarter....

One Idea per Slide

In the end, however you choose to structure the presentation, stick with One Idea per Slide. Keep the slides themselves simple, or at least as simple as possible. Even if you need to show a complex formula or equation, for example, give it space, room to breathe.

That's how you really respect your audience.

Know that your own science exceeds.
William Shakespeare, *Measure for Measure*

Training and Teaching (Classroom Presentations)

High-school, college, and post-grad teaching, along with professional training, is more than information-sharing.

You need students to retain what you're sharing – but also to interact with it, to process it, think about it, respond to it, challenge you, and go beyond what you've presented. You're changing audience thinking rather than just transferring information.

The question for this spread is not teaching or training per se, but how to use slides to support your work as a teacher/trainer.

The Deep Content

Deep content, where you're presenting it just as information, belongs in the "handouts," in quotes because in academia non-slide content usually includes assigned readings. Are you listing the kings of England? Handouts. But if you want students to remember the difference between Richard II and Richard III (and understand why there's been no Richard IV), shift into action mode. Maybe you throw out a question about Shakespeare, or show clips from Olivier's film (or Alan Alda brilliantly impersonating Olivier on a *M*A*S*H* episode), or project a picture of the Leicester car park where Richard Crookback's grave was found – but engaging your audience directly, with a visual image (still or moving) to support you, will ensure they're unlikely to mistake these two gentlemen in the future.

Plus: You already know how to teach. Ensure your slides support rather than undercut your lessons.

Slides supplement deep content. They don't deliver it.

In training as well as in higher education, you have a lot of material to cover in relatively limited time, with students across a spectrum of background information, interest levels, learning styles, and abilities. Work with your slides to engage them across as many degrees of that spectrum as you can – by getting them out of reading mode and into a combination of listening and participating.

Bullet points feel productive because they are seductive. There's clear information on the screen. The students are exposed to it. Therefore, they must be getting it.

And some immediate post-class surveys superficially suggest they do get it. However, surveys of learning taken further down the road do not support the effectiveness (putting training into practice) of bullet-point lectures.

Students are likely to retain more with One Idea per Slide, one clear idea that everyone can focus on, supported by the presenter with more information, questions, stories, interaction, and more. Of course a good teacher can generate all of that from a morass of onscreen text as well, but why epxend the additional work to overcome difficult slides?

Again, the problem isn't bullet points per se, but jumbled, text-heavy slides trying to cover too much and do too much. You can do One Idea per Slide with stock PowerPoint bullets, but it's hard to resist the pull of "oh, just let me get one more thing on this slide." Working with formats that minimize that tendency makes your job as a teacher easier in the long run, because you have increased opportunity to have the students focused on you and your ideas rather than a screen.

Tell sad stories of the death of kings.
William Shakespeare, *Richard ## II*

Decision-Support Presentations

In the business world, often your job is to present multiple alternatives to the decision-maker(s), with or without stumping for your own preferences.

To make these presentations work, you need to understand – to the extent you can – who will actually make the decision, their needs, any hot buttons to avoid, and their knowledge gaps. You also need to understand what they expect of you: Absolute mastery of your subject? An even-handed report? A favored alternative with defensible reasons? An open discussion, or confirmation of a decision already reached (one with which you might disagree)?

When the Decision Is Up for Discussion

Decide whether you want to present each alternative as a whole or go through each feature/proof point and show how the alternatives compare on that point. The former approach usually leads to clearer discussions about the overall impact of the decision. The latter might be better in the few cases where the real issues can be quantified (e.g., cost or performance is the governing factor).

Either way, keep the slides simple. The goal is to get to the actual discussion of alternatives, and their impact on the organization, as quickly as possible. For example, the set of slides on the facing page sketches one reasonable approach to a decision-support presentation, divided by candidate rather than feature. Keep in mind that the point of these slides is to facilitate a discussion (whether or not the outcome is in doubt), not convey every bit of data.

Plus: These meetings are your chance to shine. You need to *know* the details, not read them from slides.

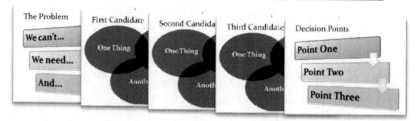

You could easily use bullet points in the slides above rather than graphical list alternatives (p. 88), right? Isn't this exactly the kind of presentation that cries out for bullet points?

Consider – what does the graphical format force you to do?

Right. You cannot squeeze a bunch of text into each list item, neither into the ovals for the candidates nor the signposts for the problem and issues. Text is for you to speak, to elaborate on as the circumstances of the meeting require. The list items simply serve as reminders for each point – to you as presenter, perhaps, but mostly to the attendees, providing a context for the details of the discussion.

You might add one more slide to cover the "minimum bar" or due diligence you've required of each candidate – e.g., their business is stable, the software runs on our network, we've checked references. (It doesn't hurt to get this out of the way early, to leave no doubt as to your own competence in running the program. If the decision makers know and trust you, you can simply speak to this work before describing the first candidate. Otherwise, it might be worth including as a reminder should they read the deck outside the presentations.)

Whern the Decision Has Been Made

If the decision has already been made (whether acknowledged or not) and your presentation is mere dumbshow, this is not the right venue to fight for your choice. Present the alternatives as above, more than ever sticking to the high points.

With due decision, make us know what we shall say we have.
William Shakespeare, *Macbeth*

Example: The Gallup Measures of Employee Engagement

Let me end this section with a personal anecdote about wrestling a difficult, dense slide into shape.

When I teach management and leadership skills, I often call on the Gallup index of employee engagement, twelve agree/disagree statements that measure how employees feel about work. For a year, this was the most frustrating slide in all of my active decks.

It contained twelve points, ranging from seven to fifteen words. The Gallup statements are valuable as additional "proof points" for what I've been teaching, but I don't want to spend much time on them. (I'm not teaching the survey, selling for Gallup, etc.)

So I had a slide with a dozen items that, because of their length, couldn't take any useful form other than text bullet points. With some formatting tricks, I could make the text large enough to read from the back, but... so what? I didn't want to read them aloud. Aside from the fact that doing so would have been seriously boring, they were a minor idea, not the focus of the session. But I did want the audience to think about them for a few seconds, and then we would discuss one or two specific issues in the list.

I tried reading just a few of them, but that led to the cognitive dissonance I've mentioned earlier between listening and reading – exacerbated by the fact each person in the audience was likely reading a different item to themselves.

I dropped it from a few sessions, but I missed the value it added.

> **Plus:** Each time we present, each time we create slides, we can incorporate lessons from past experiences.

My Solution

I finally moved the list to my "workbook," a second set of hand-outs (the first contains three-to-a-page slides) with exercises, templates, and more. (This move also let me properly credit Gallup instead of having yet more text fighting for screen real estate.)

Now I can ask the attendees to read it quickly and pick *one* item on the list that stands out, for whatever reason. I ask them to speak up with which-item-and-why after about fifteen seconds. Depending on time and attendee proclivities, I can:

- Take a few comments and move on.
- Encourage them to engage each other in discussions.
- Ask for a story of a disengaged employee (or tell a carefully redacted one myself if I'm dealing with a group cautious about sharing such things in front of each other).
- Point out one item that applies particularly well to the discussions we've had the past few hours on moving from management to leadership.

Now I've progressed from a clunky bullet-point slide – the last remaining actual-bullet-points slide in my active decks – to a clean slide containing only the text "Gallup Survey" set over the neon exclamation point I use in that deck to mark a group exercise.

I tell the story of this relatively unimportant slide for two reasons:

1. Even an experienced presenter committed to getting rid of bullet points can sometimes be stumped. I kept using the slide because ugly-and-awkward still trumped not using it. Likewise, if you can't find a better solution to a given slide than bullet points, don't feel you're letting yourself down.
2. Decks evolve over time. We reserve the right to wake up smarter every day. Keep improving your slides!

We are impressed, and engaged.
William Shakespeare, *Henry IV, pt. 1*

Five Takeaways

1. Sales presentations: You need to tell a clear story, with emphasis on the *you* and the *story*. Don't litter the slides with what you want to say. Rather, use them as part of figuring out what customer's problem and then show how you'll solve it.

2. Fiscal reviews: The focus needs to be on you and the on the data, probably in that order. The audience should have very little focus on the slides (other than as we-are-here placeholders or for highlighting key data points). Unless you're simply walking through an ossified ritual, they need to hear – and you need to share – your interpretation of why you are where you are, along with future plans. Numbers can cement your deal, but they can't inspire by themselves.

3. Scientific papers needn't be replicated on screen. Even within standard formats, find ways to engage the audience by keeping your slides out of the way.

4. Teaching and training content likewise derives both authority and value from you, the teacher/trainer. Your slides aren't the authority; you are.

5. Decision making: Don't let the slides bog down in details. Use them to keep the meeting on track. Know and/or have the details at hand, maybe even in supplementary slides (see branching, p. 156), but simple slides with one idea each can help drive out the real factors supporting the decision.

Next Steps/Action Items

- If you're engaged in one of the presentation types of this chapter, consider reworking all or part of it using One Idea per Slide. Even if it's a presentation you'll never give again, spend a few minutes with it at least thinking about how it might look using the precepts of this book. Maybe take one or two overbusy slides and rework those, focusing not on formatting or graphics but on getting them down to One Idea per Slide.

- Next time you give a presentation that falls into one of these areas, be brave. You don't have to eat the elephant in one bite, but at least take one section and explore how simplifying the slides can help your own presentation come alive.

What have you now to present?
William Shakespeare, *Timon of Athens*

I'll
by a SIGN
give
NOTICE.

VISIBLE STRUCTURE AND SIGNPOSTS.

MAPS FOR THE AUDIENCE.

The New York City Subway. The MTA in Boston. The London Underground, the Paris Metro. They all have maps and signposts to help riders understand where they are and get where they're going. Let's learn from their expertise.

Introductions and "About" Slides

It's said that the most important portion of an interview is the first minute. People choose whether or not to read a novel based on whether the first page hooks them. Real estate agents preach "curb appeal," wooing potential buyers on first impressions.

What's the first impression of the majority of standalone presentations (e.g., those outside the context of a business meeting, ongoing class, etc.)?

The speaker's introduction.

The concept is a good one. Establish the speaker's bona fides, boost the audience's belief that the presentation will help them, and provide you, the speaker, with a running start.

Great concept. The execution rarely measures up.

Introductions Delivered by Someone Else

I have sat through literally hundreds of introductions written by (or on behalf of) the speaker and delivered verbatim by someone else. Sometimes the introducer was a person of power and prestige – a BigLaw managing partner, a CEO, a politician. More often, the reader was a session organizer, often known to only a few audience members.

In every case I can recall, the energy in the room *dropped* during introductions read off a piece of paper. (Freeform introductions by a person of note are a different story… and a rare one.)

Plus: Create a separate brief introduction specific to each audience.

Indeed, many speakers have practiced lines for dealing with these introductions, e.g., "Thank you for reading that just the way my mother wrote it." A good line can get the energy and focus back on track... but why lose it in the first place?

Prepare a two-sentence preamble and ask that person to use it rather than, say, the formal biography submitted for the conference program. Capture one *brief* career highlight relevant to the audience, along with one – also brief – reason your presentation will be meaningful to attendees. (And include the pronunciation of your name if there is any chance someone will stumble over it or mangle it.) Read it aloud multiple times, until you are sure that it flows smoothly and takes less than twenty seconds. Even at a professional conference, where people care about curricula vitae, leave the details to the conference program. Connecting with the audience is too important to sidetrack the first two minutes.

Note what's not included: The title or subject of your presentation. Because that's redundant. It's on your title slide, which presumably is showing on screen, and it's the reason most of the audience is in the room. Then launch into your presentation.

Somewhere in the first few minutes, once you've captured the audience attention, you can begin to work in a few other items of your biography relevant to the audience, as noted below.

Crafting Your Own Introduction

Your most important introduction is *you* – your voice, your energy, and your ability to make the audience listen to you rather than get lost reading your slides. That first impression beats most anything others will say about you. If the audience needs to know more about you, weave it into your first five minutes.

What you've done may matter to the audience – but now, in the room, not as much as what you're doing, how you're connecting.

> *Say his name, good friend.*
> William Shakespeare, *Cymbeline*

Agendas and Other Signposts

Longer presentations – say, those over thirty or forty minutes – benefit from itineraries and signposts (p. 84), e.g., a rolling agenda (sketched below, say slides 3, 11, and 17) or section headings.

Itineraries (rolling agendas) for your presentation as a whole do more than supply a you-are-here message. They provide a context – "here's how what I've talked about so far fits into the bigger picture." Implied by that context is, "More good stuff is coming soon." In addition, they map a sane exit-and-reentry strategy for someone who has to make a critical phone call or take a bio-break.

Along those lines, they serve yet another critical purpose:

Helping Those Who've "Zoned Out" Find Their Way Back In

What happens when an attendee loses the thread of your presentation, whether because they've zoned out, they've been distracted, or they're worrying an ongoing issue? Do you want to keep excluding them, or do you want to help them find their way back to your content? Itineraries and signposts provide an easy reentry path to reconnect with you and your subject matter.

Plus: A rolling agenda uses colors, arrows, etc. to show attendees where they are in the presentation.

(By the way, not all distractions are bad. It's not great news if attendees are bored, but what about attendees with a boiling issue they need to deal with? Their choice is either to stay away or to attend your presentation and pick spots during it to respond to the external problem. Or perhaps someone's not paying attention because you've helped him uncover an insight that he's now busy sorting through, figuring out how to apply it to a current issue. I'd call either of these last two scenarios a "win" for the presenter and the presentation.)

Long Days and Lead-Ins

For presentations with breaks, such as training sessions, provide a reentry path after each break. A signpost is a good start, but it can be helpful to offer more to transition them back into the mood and feel of the presentation.

In a sense, each return-from-break portion of your presentation needs its own first and second slides, as noted below and in the next spread.

In longer presenations, it can be hard to predetermine where the breaks will occur. Some groups are simply more interactive than others, or express different interests. I try to keep a spare set of agenda and "second" slides I can cobble together if I need to break in an unanticipated spot, but even without these, I can make sure that I as a speaker deliver this content "off the cuff."

Which leads us to the next heading. What's this Second Slide about? What's the purpose (p. 76) of your Second Slide, whether second in the presentation or second in a section after a break?

The Agenda Is Not Your Second Slide

See the following spread.

Read this schedule.
William Shakespeare, *Julius Caesar*

Your Second Slide

The first slide in your presentation is your title slide. The first slide after a break in a longer presentation should generally be a signpost or itinerary, as noted on the preceding spread. Does that mean the Second Slide overall should be an agenda?

No.

Boring. And worse than boring – you're squandering an opportunity to engage the audience and raise the excitement level for the presentation.

The Purpose of the Second Slide

The title/first slide is housekeeping – necessary, but, like speaker introductions (p. 138), best when gotten out of the way quickly.

The Second Slide must ratchet up audience involvement, whether interactive involvement or engagement in your subject. It doesn't even have to be a slide with content.

For example, when I lecture about the reasons projects fail, my Second Slide may be a picture of the Fukushima nuclear reactor, or the Challenger coming apart, or Boston's "Big Dig" (which I'm about to replace with my local – Seattle – tunnel mess). No title, just a picture. I'll give a verbal "title" and ask, "So why did this project fail?" I want to get a conversation going among the attendees (which got extra interesting the afternoon I had someone who'd worked on Fukushima). Three or four minutes of discussion makes clear that most project failures consist of multiple, cascading problems that the team failed to address – and often blew off as "not gonna happen." The audience has made my key point for me – and in a way they'll remember.

> **Plus:** If you're not comfortable yet with audience inter-
> action, at least jump to the meat of your content.

Other good Second Slides include demonstrations, high-stakes statements of the problem, brief exercises (a terrific choice if attendees are sitting at tables and can interact with each other but effective even in standard seating arrangements), *brief* and highly relevant stories, "what if" rhetorical questions, the "one thing" I guarantee you'll learn today, or references to relevant contemporary events.

Use your imagination.

Just don't get bogged down in temporizing, in content that doesn't reach out and grab your audience, content such as agendas, "about the speaker" slides, or housekeeping (breaks and bathrooms).

As noted on the preceding spread, when the audience returns from breaks, you should have a "Second Slide" ready, even if it's not an actual slide – something to get them refocused, get their energy back up, reconnect you with them. (This step is doubly critical after a lunch break, to avoid a postprandial slump.)

Second Slides at Business Meetings

It's easy to see how the ideas above play out for conference sessions, training, and so on. But what about business meetings?

For all but the most structured business meetings (e.g., budget reviews whose minute-by-minute format is predefined), Second Slides still have value – even if you do them without an actual slide dedicated to that purpose. For example, consider the request for funding of Bad Example #1 (p. 30) and the revision of its opening suggested on p. 80. The revision actually offers a pair of "Second Slides" – a statement of the underlying business problem followed by "We compete with Google," in effect a rhetorical question (with the question "We *do*?" forming in the audience's mind). You'll get to facts and figures soon enough – but your first step is to connect with the audience, getting early buy-in to your message.

Let me have audience for a word or two. I am the second.
William Shakespeare, *As You Like It*

Five Takeaways

1. Itineraries, and signposts help the audience find their way into and within a presentation.

2. Itineraries (rolling agendas) and signposts (topic/section headings) also provide smooth reentry for attendees who've lost focus, whether because of distractions, zoning out, stepping away, etc.

3. Keep introductions short. Very short.

4. Your "Second Slide" should grab the audience, pulling them into the presentation and connecting them with the core idea.

5. After each break in an extended presentation, provide a signpost for reentry and a Second Slide to rebuild energy and focus – even if these are delivered verbally rather than with purpose-built slides.

Next Steps/Action Items

- Get rid of introductions, "about the speaker" slides, and so on from your existing presentations – at least those you might reuse.

- Work up a Second Slide for at least a few of those presentations.

- Write up an introduction of no more than two sentences and thirty words. This can become the core that you rework for each particular presentation at which you're introduced.

I'll by a sign give notice.
William Shakespeare, *Henry VI pt. 1*

Important
and
most SERIOUS
DESIGNS.

DESIGN
MODE.

MAKE YOUR SLIDES LOOK TERRIFIC – EVEN IF YOU'RE NOT AN ARTIST.

It takes little artistic talent to create good-looking slides. Artistry can help move the needle from good to great, but we can go from yecch to good with a few simple techniques and some attention to detail.

Configuring PowerPoint

The Quick-Access Toolbar

Microsoft Office products – PowerPoint, Word, etc. – have at the top a customizable row of icons offering instant access to almost all of the menu commands – and some that aren't on the menus.

When you install these tools, the icons are bland, largely useful for inexperienced users (who often don't even realize they're there): **Save**, **Undo**, **Redo**, etc.

Replace or supplement them with a more useful set, ones that will help you move quickly through the work of creating better slides.

Here's an annotated set I've been using, along with a link to a page on my website (SlideStrong.com/qat) from which you can download this toolbar and others.

Format Painter: To make Thing B look like Thing A (whether a graphic or text), click on Thing A, click the **Format Painter**, then click on Thing B, instead of trying to figure out what font you used or the color or how thick the object outline is.

Crop graphics by cutting off areas you don't want, just as you would for a photograph.

Plus: This toolbar is not just for power users. It's the fastest way to make PowerPoint map your own needs.

Insert Picture from the web. Type in what you're looking for.

Selection Pane: Useful when you have a bunch of overlapping graphics. You can "turn off" various graphics so you can click on those "beneath" them. This is an advanced tool, but worthwhile – and hard to discover – if you use lots of pictures.

Animation Pane: Lists all of the animation effects in a given slide, letting you rearrange them, configure them, and so on. Complex animation is best reserved for special cases, but it can be effective (e.g., the "opening doors" list on p. 88).

Collapse Element: This and the next three icons are active in **Outline View** (pp. 109 and 190). This icon collapses a nested outline set to only the highest level.

Collapse All outline elements to the top levels (= slide titles).

Expand Element, Expand All – the opposite of Collapse.

Highlighter: Useful for highlighting numbers or data elements (p. 124) because it looks like hand-done highlighting with a yellow marker (or whatever color you choose).

All of these live within PowerPoint menus or by right-clicking *somewhere*, but who wants to waste time menu-surfing for obscure commands – or even not-so-obscure commands that are on a menu tab different from the one currently displayed? It's much faster and easier to put such commands on this **Quick Access Toolbar**.

I urge you to experiment with this power-user tool. Start with one of my toolbars, then add your own commands. Click the down-arrow at the right of the toolbar, select **More Commands**, and then click **Import/Export** at the bottom of the dialog box, the same dialog box that then lets you add and rearrange your own commands.

Take you to your tools.
William Shakespeare, *Titus Andronicus*

"Bullet" Lists

Here, repeated in miniature from p. 88, are a dozen different, simple alternatives to bullet lists.

Yes, simple (mostly). Eleven were created directly in PowerPoint with knowledge of the software but little effort. The twelfth, the opening doors, also uses only PowerPoint but includes complex animation to offer an example of what's possible. (Many such animations and images are available on line.)

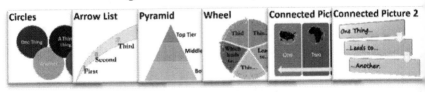

The six examples above use **Smart Art**. On the first four, I typed the list items separately (see the note on p. 88) for more control over positioning and font size. The last two use text typed directly into the **Smart Art** control.

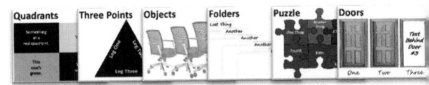

The next six examples are graphics – first two simple PowerPoint shapes, followed by a picture of my office chair, and then three pictures available on the web (or in earlier versions of Power-Point), each of the pictures repeated two or more times. Only animating the doors to rotate open is difficult – but I doubt anyone would be disappointed if you simplified this animation, fading **out** each door to reveal the text below it.

Plus: Start with simple Smart Art for your first new-style bullet lists, without sweating format, font size, etc.

Could they look better? Of course. (For one thing, they're not black-and-white in "real life.") But my goal for each of these was to see what I could create in less than sixty seconds for each image (doors and puzzle excepted, which come from my working decks).

Consider what these kinds of lists do for a presentation:

- The audience gets a visually interesting list.
- The format forces you to simplify each list item – say, one to three words – so that the bulk of the information comes from you rather than the screen.
- You can show relationships among list items (e.g., the wheel, the pyramid, the arrow, etc.).
- You can enrich the list via metaphor (e.g., doors, puzzle).

Here's how a metaphor idea can strengthen the idea behind a slide.

The doors recall Monty Hall and *Let's Make a Deal*, and I explicitly refer to them as Door #1, etc. In a time management course, I might say, "Let's say you respond to every email the instant it hits your inbox. What do you get? Monty, show us what's behind Door #1." Click, and Door #1 reveals, say, a stressed office worker drowning in paper. Doors #2 and #3 reflect other choices. My slide says, in effect, "You can control being overwhelmed," reinforcing visually the point I'm making.

Likewise, a puzzle list suggests 1) if you put these pieces together properly, you'll find the answer and 2) you *can* do it, because you can solve puzzles. The folders are one of the few visual images I've found for more than six or seven items on a list, but it's an effective metaphor only for knowledge-worker or professional audiences (e.g., not a good match to the Bill of Rights list, p. 87).

It's no harder to use simple **Smart Art** for bullet lists than to type them – and they'll look better, engage the audience, and perhaps inspire you to consider improved ways to present a given list.

See the lists, and all things fit.
William Shakespeare, *Henry VI pt. 2*

Formatting Smart Art

PowerPoint's **Smart Art** is an extremely powerful tool for improving your presentation in two ways:

- Visually demonstrate the relationship of items to each other – e.g., steps in a process – without requiring artistic skill.
- Provide a visually pleasing alternative to bullet lists.

Unfortunately, the default settings of Smart Art objects have one characteristic that can work against effective presentations: the text resizes as you type, so that it's hard to create readably large type for all but the simplest words.

I'm all in favor of shortening concepts, trying to get them down to a single word where possible. However, even those single words are often long enough to cause Smart Art to resize the text to 18 points or below, too small for easy reading on screen. Here are two ways to fix this problem.

Text Box Margins

Most Smart Art objects keep the text 0.25 inches from each side of the invisible **text box** that holds the words. For many objects, however, there's no reason that the text can't take up a greater proportion of the object.

To fix, right-click on one of the words in a "list item" and select **Format Shape**. Then click **Text Options** and then the **Text Box** button (an icon of a mini-document). Change the **Left** and **Right Margins** to zero. Unfortunately, you need to do this separately for each text box in the **Smart Art** object. I keep a store of these, in a separate slide deck, already "fixed" in this manner. When I need one, I grab it from there and **copy/paste** it into my presentation.

Plus: You can use Smart Art as is, or let it create the graphics over which you add your own text.

Overlay the Text Manually

A second solution – more work, but usually offering better results – is to keep the text separate from the **Smart Art**. Use **Smart Art** to create a graphical element. Then lay the text on top of it manually, as follows:

Create your **Smart Art** using a single space (press the spacebar) for each textual element or list item, creating a placeholder or "bullet" for that element. Now, for each list item:

- Insert a **text box** (on the **Insert** menu, click **Text Box**).
- Type your text.
- Resize it (the default, 18 point, is too small for great slides) via the **Font** tab of the **Home** menu.
- Use the mouse to drag it into position.
- Change the font and color as needed and consider **Bold** and **Text Shadow**, all found on the **Font** tab of the **Home** menu.

The downside is that if you change your **Smart Art**, the text remains where it was. I recommend you use this method only after you're convinced you have a usable graphic from the **Smart Art** and your only remaining problem is text sizing/positioning.

Note that most of the **Smart Art**-based "list" slides on the Better Lists spread (pp. 88 and 150) use this method.

Character Spacing

PowerPoint's default Calibri font already fits lots of letters into small spaces compared to, say, Garamond (this book's text font). Still, you can sometimes squeeze it further. Click the tiny arrow at the lower right of the **Font** tab, then click **Character Spacing** and select **Condensed**. The larger the font, the more you can condense it. Just don't go overboard. Subtle, subtle, subtle, please.

Yea, and text underneath.
William Shakespeare, *Much Ado About Nothing*

Inserting Images

The Internet is brimming with useful, interesting images. (It's not all cat videos and political rants.)

You can search within PowerPoint by clicking **Online Pictures** on the **Insert** menu. However, you get a limited selection, without licensing information. If you're presenting in a public forum or even in many private situations, you must be sure you can use the image. (Consult a legal advisor for more details. It's complicated.)

Image size ▾ Color ▾ Type ▾ Layout ▾ People ▾ Date ▾	License ▾

	All
However, if you use your browser to	
search bing.com/images (Microsoft's	Public domain
image search engine), you'll see a	
small menu bar just above the array	Free to share and use
of images, with the item *License* near	
the end. Click *License*, and you'll be	Free to share and use commercially
able to filter the images according to	
those the copyright owners have	Free to modify, share, and use
made available for your use.	
	Free to modify, share, and use commercially
	Learn more

Click the *Learn more* menu item for further information on how you can use these images.

Your organization may have a license from an organization such as Shutterstock or Getty Images/iStockPhoto, or you can purchase licenses as an individual user – or for a specific photo. Millions of free images are also available from Flickr, Creative Commons, and Wikimedia commons – but I recommend you get help understanding the licensing terms for these images. ("Free" means no cost, not that you can use them for all purposes.)

> **Plus:** Images add so much power to your slides that it's worth learning how to find and position them.

The easiest images to use are professional shots on a white background – which is easily removed within PowerPoint. Click the image and select **Remove Background** on the **Format** menu. Adjust the cropping rectangle around your image first. Then, if needed, use the **Mark Areas to Keep** or **Mark Areas to Remove** tools to click on areas that PowerPoint didn't recognize appropriately. Simple images, especially those with white backgrounds or clear separation between the figure and the background, usually offer the easiest cleanup.

Animals in natural settings tend to be the hardest, but sometimes, you simply need an elephant to make a point. (That said, it may be easier to find another image, even if you have to pay for one rather than spend half an hour fighting with image processing.)

Cleanup doesn't have to be perfect. The less time your image is visible, or the smaller it is, the less the audience will notice imperfections.

Images and Colored Backgrounds

It's hard to place images on colored backgrounds unless you're using them as is (rectangular, without cutouts). Once you start cutting out stuff you don't want, you need to remove all said stuff to let your slide's background show through. So until you get practiced at these techniques (or find someone to help), choose simple images – or allow them to occupy the entire screen.

Full-Screen Images

The most powerful images usually occupy the full screen, sometimes with your title or other information superimposed on them. These rarely need **Remove Background** or other complex processing. Use a **Title-Only Layout** (see the next spread), or a **Blank Layout** over which you **Insert** a **Text Box**.

The image of it gives me content.
William Shakespeare, *Measure for Measure*

Layouts

PowerPoint supports a number of different "looks" for each slide, called **Layouts**. If you click **Layout** on the **Home** menu (or one any of the right-click menus), you'll see something like this:

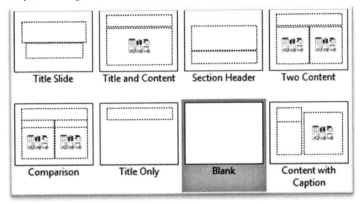

Each of these shows a different way to lay out your slides.

By default, a new presentation starts with the **Title Slide layout**, and subsequent slides use the **Title and Content layout**. But they're not your only options. In fact, you'll likely create better looking slides if you maximize use of the **Title Only** and even **Blank layouts** after your **Title Slide**. ("**Title Only**" is not a **Title Slide** but rather contains only a box for a slide header/title.)

Whenever you **Insert** a **New Slide**, PowerPoint defaults to the **layout** of the preceding slide unless you click the text beneath the **New Slide** icon – which brings up the **Layout** tab shown above. Each PowerPoint **theme** has a different look for these **layouts**. Each **theme** has a **Title and Content layout**, for example, but it will look different in the blue "Slice" **theme** than it does in the utilitarian gray "Office" **theme** pictured above.

> **Plus:** Understanding **layouts** and the **Master View** will make PowerPoint a lot easier to use.

Changing Layouts of Existing Slides

You can change the layout of a slide via right-click. Select **Layout** and choose from among the options on the **Layout** tab. Take a minute to experiment with different layouts. You won't lose any existing text; PowerPoint will put it in a **text box** if, for example, you convert to a **Blank layout**. (**Undo** is your friend.)

Use the mouse to reposition the title of one of your **Title and Content** slides. Now click **Layout** and select **Title and Content**, and the title will return to its original position. You can also use **Reset** (**Slides** portion of the **Home** menu) to force any position or font changes to match the default **layout** for that slide..

Why Layouts Matter

Layouts allow you to unify the look and feel of your slides.

For example, let's say you've been working with the green-on-white "Facet" **theme** used in Bad Example #1 (p. 30) when you discover the presentation will be given in a dark room. Having read p. 110, you know that light text on a dark background is easier to read in such rooms. You can either rework all of your slides, or you can simple browse the **Design** menu and choose a dark-background theme. If you've used **layouts** rather than plunking stuff down at random on your slides, with one click all of your slides will be adjuted to work with the new **theme**.

This property of **layouts** becomes especially important when you set up the **Master View** (next spread).

Okay, stop reading for a minute. Open PowerPoint. Go try this stuff. Poke around with a duplicate copy of one of your decks to understand how **layouts** work. Just reading it here isn't enough.

You lay out too much.
William Shakespeare, *Cymbeline*

Master of PowerPoint

The true "master" of PowerPoint is the **Slide Master** (on the **View** menu).

The master slides, one for each **Layout** (preceding spread), determine how your slides will look:

- **Font** name, size, and color for each element, such as the slide title, slide content, etc.
- **Background Color** for each of the elements.
- **Footers** such as dates and page numbers (avoid these for onscreen use except in certain situations, such as a business meeting where attendees are following along in their own copies).
- **Slide Backgrounds** including background graphics.

Modifying the Slide Master accomplishes three things:

1. Your slides will have a unified look.
2. If you want to, say, change fonts, change the master and the changes will ripple through your slides automatically.
3. You won't have to fix overly small fonts on each slide.

Of these, the last is by far the most important.

PowerPoint's Tiny Fonts

Because PowerPoint layouts default to bullet-points-with-lots-and-lots-of-text, most **Title and Content** layouts start with smallish fonts for the highest bullet-point level and decrease from there. In theory, 18-point fonts are legible in most rooms… but legible isn't the same thing as "begging to be read."

With One Idea per Slide, there's no reason to use small fonts.

Plus: When you're done modifying your masters, click **Close Master View** on the **Slide Master** menu.

Using 40-point-plus fonts affords your ideas the boldness they deserve. After all, the text on the slide doesn't represent your idea per se but is a reminder of your idea, a stand-in, a mnemonic.

Fix it on the **Theme Slide Master**, the first slide in the **Slide Master** view. (You'll probably have to scroll the left-hand window up to find it.) Click the dotted-line box around the content area, which says "Edit Master text styles"; you'll know you have it when the dotted outline turns sold. Now, on the **Home** menu, click the **Increase Font Size (A^)** icon a few times until the **Font Size** box says 40+ (or, better, 44+ or 48+).

While you've got the **Slide Master** open, let's fix two other aspects. First, right-click the content area and select **Format Shape** to open

a window at right. At the top of that window, click **Text Options**, and then click the icon below it showing a **text box** (left). Now, click the **Do not Autofit** button. If your text grows too lengthy, the box will expand, rather than forcing your text down a size. You want this as a warning you're trying to squeeze in too much text. (If you absolutely have to do so, change the size manually for that slide.)

Second, now that you've enlarged the body text, you might want to make the slide titles stronger as well. Click the dotted line around the title area until it turns solid. Now, on the **Home** menu, increase the font size to, say, 48 points. Consider making your titles **Bold** (works better for sans serif fonts such as Calibri) and **Shadowed** (the **S** icon beneath the name of the font in the menu).

Slide Background

Use the **Background** area of the **Slide Master** menu to define the background for your slides. You can choose a color scheme via **Colors**, add a **Background Style**, or import a picture (p. 154) that will underlie each of your slides. Make sure you use the first slide, called the **Theme Master**, in the left-hand window.

I'll be master of it.
William Shakespeare, *Troilus and Cressida*

Professional Slide Cleanup

Many companies and institutions have people on staff who will "polish" your slides, cleaning up any rough edges, precisely aligning text and graphics, and so on.

Some will do more, from offering suggestions about fonts and colors (useful) to reformatting your slides in the organization's standard template (not so useful, and occasionally wrong-headed).

The best way to use such a service is to work out with them, in advance, what you expect them to do – and what you expect them *not* to do.

You might start with a list such as the following:

Cleanup To-Do List:

- Fix spelling errors. If you're not sure about technical terms, please ask me first.
- Fix alignment errors within slides
- Fix misalignment of text (title and/or content) between one slide and the next. If doing so causes significant reformatting of content or font-size issues, please ask me first. Consistency takes a back seat to clarity and readability.
- Fix *obviously unintentional* inconsistencies – e.g., slight variations in text color or size.
- Fix *obviously unintentional* animation errors – e.g., three items on a slide **fade in** and the fourth **appears**.
- Fix included graphics to the extent the adjustment is straightforward – alignment, cropping, contrast, etc.

Plus: Cleanup does not make slides more effective, but it can make them a bit easier to read.

Please Do Not Make These Changes:

- Do not change the **layout** of slides beyond issues on the to-do list such as alignment errors.
- Do not force the slides to conform to some template other than the one I'm currently using.
- Do not force a slide to conform to the current template unless there is an obvious error. If you're not sure, please ask first.
- Do not remove or alter speaker notes.
- Do not add **animations** or **transitions** unless I've requested them for a particular slide.
- Do not allow **Autofit** to alter the size of text.

Please Offer to Discuss/Help With These Items (But Do Not Change Them Until We've Talked):

- Determine the best fonts for the presentation.
- Determine the best colors for the presentation.
- Find better/cleaner images (graphics) than the ones I'm currently using.

You can find this list online via the QR code at right.

"Amateur" Slide Cleanup

Sometimes when you're part of a group presentation, such as a panel discussion at a conference, someone in the group will volunteer to take charge of the slide deck.

That's okay, but discuss with them first what they'll do — and what you would prefer they leave alone. The most important point is to ensure that your clear, crisp presentation, with One Idea per Slide, remains so.

Wipe his tables clean.
William Shakespeare, *Henry IV pt. 2*

Branching: Jumping to a Given Slide

There are three reasons you may want to jump to a specific slide:

1. Someone asks a question that another slide (or group of slides) answers effectively.
2. You need to cut out part of your presentation, either because time is growing short or you realize it doesn't speak to your audience.
3. You want to pull in extra or optional material.

The first reason is tricky and often leads to awkward fumbling, unless you have a printout of your slides/slide numbers. Even so, you're likely to have to jump ahead, jump back to where you were, and then when you reach that part in your deck, skip over it the second time. It's usually better to defer the discussion, saying, "We'll cover that later."

Skip/Jump to a Slide, Impromtu Style

In **Presenter View** (with your computer showing your notes rather than what's projected), click the **See all slides** icon. (In older

versions, they're already visible at the bottom of the screen.) Scroll to the slide you want, if necessary, and then click it. It will appear on screen.

If you know the slide number, type the number on the keyboard and hit Enter. This method works even when the laptop has the same display as the projected screen rather than **Presenter View** (p. 176). However, you have to know your slide numbers.

> **Plus:** I sometimes put a red dot in the corner of slides to remind me that I can branch off from that slide.

Jump to an Optional "Sub-Show"

When I teach time management, some audiences want to learn to run meetings better, while others have no control over them. For the former audiences, I jump to a section of my deck about meeting management. When that section ends, my slides continue automatically where I left off. There's no fumbling at the monitor or keyboard, just a single mouse click (or touchscreen contact). If I Click/touch the people in the slide at right, we go to the Meetings section. Otherwise, the clicker takes me to the next slide.

It's a two-step process: set up a **Custom Slide Show**, and then create a link to it.

First, identify the slides you want and put them at the end of your deck. Now, on the **Slide Show** menu, choose **Custom Slide Show**. Click **New** in the dialog box that appears, choose a name (e.g., *Meetings*), select and **Add** the appropriate slides, and press OK.

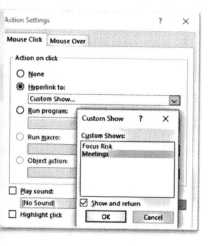

Now go to the slide you want to branch (jump) from. Select the object you want to click on – which can include any of the text elements on the page, not just a graphic. On the **Insert** menu, select **Action**, then choose **Hyperlink** to **Custom Show**. You'll see a dialog box like the one at left. Choose your custom show. Check **Show and return** for a "digression," like my Meetings scenario. Leave it blank if you're creating easy ways to omit some slides.

This fierce abridgement hath to it circumstantial branches.
William Shakespeare, *Cymbeline*

Encouraging Questions During the Presentation

Different speakers have different philosophies on whether you should take questions *during* the presentation or ask the audience to wait for the end.

Overall, your choice depends on your own style, the format of your session, and the audience itself. (I personally encourage questions during the presentation except for keynote-type speeches to larger audiences... where my own hearing loss comes into play, preventing it from being a smooth experience.)

Let's assume you decide to encourage questions during the presentation. (See also the spread on audience participation, p. 180.) How do you make it work?

"Any Questions?" – Not!

What happens if you ask, "Any questions so far?" Most of the time you get a sea of dull head-nodding. Occasionally someone will ask a question that's invariably off topic – because they think you're begging for a question and they're either trying to help or just want to hear themselves talk.

Rather, find spots in your presentation where you want to engage with the audience. Perhaps you're delivering a scientific paper or a business request and want their input. Perhaps you're teaching and know that engaged students learn and retain more.

Plus: Good questions can both engage the audience and help move them toward your point of view.

At that point, ask the kind of question that demands a response:

- Do you think we're all seeing the broadest selection of great candidates (Bad Example #1, p. 30)?
- Why did Pickett's charge fail?
- How does this research touch on work you're doing in your own fields?
- Why do directors keep including Middleton's additions to *Macbeth* (Bad Example #2, p. 32)?

Note that all but the first are open-ended questions, which is usually the right format for provoking discussion. (The first question, as part of a funding request, is designed to get the audience to agree subconsciously that we need the new software… and in my experience will probably lead to significant "off-topic" discussion, which I would encourage because it validates the fact that we indeed have the problem my proposal purports to fix.)

While good teachers are used to asking these questions throughout their presentation, many of us find it foreign and, under the pressure of presenting, forget (or fear) to do so. Thus you many find it useful to build "question" slides right into your deck.

There's value in using a consistent format for question slides, both to cue the audience and as a reminder to yourself. You don't need to do this, of course. Rather it offers another tool that helps you overcome presentation anxiety.

If you include question slides, note one other advantage to asking open-ended rather than yes/no questions. If you have an audience reluctant to participate, or if you're running short on time, you can treat the questions as rhetorical and answer them yourself.

I will not stay thy questions.
William Shakespeare, *A Midsummer Night's Dream*

Handouts

The best way to communicate large amounts of data is not by displaying it on screen, rows of squinty type lost among more rows.

Give the data to your audience in a form they can easily read, on paper (or electronically), as handouts.

PowerPoint offers a number of handout formats. For classes, seminars, etc., consider three-to-a-page as a good starting point, since the format offers room to take notes opposite each slide. When I'm teaching, I want the audience to make notes, since the key points will come from me and what I say, not from the words on the slides.

On the other hand, when I do keynote presentations, I generally provide very limited handouts – because I want the audience focused on my words, and because keynote addresses aren't usually designed to be information-dense. I'm trying to change minds, to communicate ideas, and handouts don't carry the same impact. I'll often set up separate handouts to meet conference requirements – a handful of key slides, plus notes, references, a bibliography, etc.

If you want to provide slides and aren't expecting attendees to take notes (or you know the handouts will be distributed electronically only), go with the default six-to-a-page setup.

The easiest way to create handouts is to **Save As** PDF format, which brings up an **Options** button for controlling the layout of the results.

Plus: Handouts, if you use them, are important in determining how your presentation is received.

Remember to ensure that an appropriate copyright notice appears on your handouts. Consider putting it on the footer of each page: on the **View** menu, select **Handout Master** and type your copyright notice. You may need to make the footer longer. Click the dotted-line border until the round **handles** appear, and then drag the right or left **handle** to enlarge the box.

Handouts That Aren't Duplicated On Screen

I've written in a number of places in this book about the futility of displaying large amounts of data on screen, and suggested that in many cases you avoid showing the data sheets entirely, using the onscreen slide to serve up a focus point, a data highlight, etc.

But if it's not on screen, how do you include the data in a handout? Let's explore two ways to accomplish this minor feat.

Separate Handouts: If you don't have to include the data sheets in your main handout, why not create a separate data handout?

In fact, I do this all the time with my long-form seminars, where I offer copies of the handouts as well as a separate workbook that contains exercises – and a few longer lists ill-suited to screen display. Attendees can have the handout open to the current slide while also focusing on the exercise or data.

Hidden Slides can be set to print or not-print (**Save As** PDF, then **Options**). You can set up your data slides as **Hidden** by right-clicking on them in the left-hand thumbnails panel or the **Slide Sorter** view. Note that this method creates readable copies of data-dense slides only if you're distributing them as full-size pages, common in corporate settings but rarely used, say, at conferences – and generally a significant waste of paper.

My hands I'll trust.
William Shakespeare, *Antony and Cleopatra*

For Teachers: Handouts, Answers, and the "Reveal"

One of the problems with handouts is that they (usually) contain the answers to the thought-provoking questions you're asking. For example, if on Slide 14 you ask which rights are covered by the First Amendment to the U.S. Constitution, Slide 15 almost certainly has the text of the amendment. What keeps the audience from glancing at the handout to find than answer?

It's not a big deal on a factual question, since someone will probably know the answer before the laggards can look it up. But what if you've thrown out a question to provoke a discussion? For example, ask why the South failed at Gettysburg, and there are a dozen contributing factors. You don't want the audience looking ahead at your handout but rather arguing the weight to assign to J.E.B. Stuart's wild ride, Lee's micromanagement, Buford's situational awareness, even the fence halfway up Cemetery Ridge. But…

- At some point you're going to show the slide listing these dozen or so factors.
- You don't want the audience to see this material in the handouts (or on screen) during the discussion.
- You *do* want the audience to walk away with a copy of this slide in their handouts somewhere.

This is a common situation when you're teaching a seminar (in school, for business, etc.) or want to pose a discussion question. PowerPoint offers an easy, slick way to handle this scenario.

Plus: If your slide has a title, click it, then **Arrange / Bring to Front** so the title is visible on the handouts.

The trick is to place this slide in your deck twice, once where you will display it and another time for the handouts only.

You can put that second copy at the very end of the deck, after the putative end of your presentation, and thus never show it, or you can put it near the end as a reminder to attendees that it's in the handouts.

Now all you need to do is "cover up" the first copy, the one you'll reveal following the discussion.

Hiding the Slide

1. On the **Insert** menu, choose **Shapes**. Click the rectangle.
2. Drag the rectangle across your slide so that it covers the entire slide.
3. Choose a **Shape Fill** color. (Cooler but a bit more work: Right-click the rectangle and select **Format Shape**. From the list of **Fill** options in the right-hand window, select **Slide background fill**. Now your slide appears empty.)

When you print the handouts, only the rectangle will print, not the material beneath it.

Setting up the Slide Reveal

1. Select the rectangle by clicking it.
2. On the **Animations** menu, select **Add Animation** and then **Disappear** (in the **Exit** group).
3. On the **Timing** portion of **Animations**, choose **With Previous**, which for the first animation is "on load."

Now when you go to that slide, audience will see your content but won't actually see the rectangle. The slide will seem completely normal... except that it is blank in their handouts.

> *You will reveal it.*
> William Shakespeare, *Hamlet*

Computer and Slide Advancer

Wherever possible, I run my slides from my own computer. I know they work and display properly. In addition, I use my touch screen to "draw" on the slides live, such as circling key points.

Your mileage may vary, as they say.

If you're not comfortable setting up your own laptop or connecting it to a variety of projection devices, then you may well prefer to rely on the venue's computer system.

In any case, as a backup, I recommend the following:

- Email the conference organizer a copy of your slides, or use Dropbox™ or Google Docs™ or some equivalent method if it's too big to email; and…
- Save a copy to an Internet-based site – e.g., Google Docs or Microsoft OneDrive™ – where you can retrieve it if need be; and…
- Carry a copy on a flash drive (thumb drive).

Note that those are all connected by "and."

Not "or."

Overkill? Well… maybe. But stuff happens.

I'd prefer to have a variety of backup options rather than be left hanging when something breaks down.

Plus: Presenting is stressful enough. Minimize the number of things out of your control.

The Slide Advancer/"Clicker"

I am hardcore about my slide advancer, or clicker. I always, always use my own, even when logistics or circumstances force me to use the event organizer's computer. Or at least I try to use my own. Every once in a while I give a presentation on an organization's locked-down computer, where I can't install my own clicker. So I adapt. But I miss the little guy.

Even in corporate meetings, if there was any chance I'd be walking around, I used my own clicker. (If I knew I would be seated at the computer, I used the computer's arrow keys.)

There are a number of clickers that fit easily in the palm of your hand – lightweight, with few buttons to cross you up. Find one you like, and practice with it. I've even taped over the "wrong" buttons on mine, so there's no chance it will start acting like a laser pointer when I least expect it.

I suggest you avoid the clickers that look like hockey pucks. The best ones hide in your hand rather than dominate it. And don't cheap out; get one with a reputation for reliability.

Also, bring spare batteries – and know how to change the battery. It doesn't hurt to replace the battery every few uses as a preventive measure.

Test the clicker before the audience enters the room, if possible. I always try to walk around the room, clicking from behind the back row, from the corners, and so on. As noted on p. 178, I usually walk around when I speak. I want to be sure the clicker won't fail me as I stand behind the audience, encouraging them to throw out suggestions and alternatives and interact with each other.

Be advanced, and be received.
William Shakespeare, *Titus Andronicus*

Five Takeaways

The takeaways for this chapter are really action items, things to try out. Practice with them before you need them.

1. Download and/or customize a **Quick Access Toolbar**. Why hunt through menus for various tools? The **Crop** tool and **Format Painter** in particular always seem to be on the "wrong' menu when I need them.

2. **Smart Art** is a terrific feature for adding quality graphical or visual elements to your deck. Open a blank deck, create a couple of quick lists (e.g., your three favorite football players), and experiment with formatting those lists within and overlaid on top of **Smart Art**.

3. On that throwaway deck, include a slide with a few images of, say, furniture, downloaded from the web. Try **Remove Background** with one of the furniture pieces. Explore the various controls on the **Format** menu, such as **Corrections**, **Color**, and **Artistic Effects**. (Don't get carried away by the last!)

4. Create a "throwaway" deck with a **Title Slide layout**, a **Title and Content layout**, and a **Title Only layout**, adding some text to each slide. Explore the **Slide Master**. Change fonts, sizes, colors, and backgrounds, and see how they affect your slides.

5. Make a copy of an existing deck. Turn the last five slides into a **Custom Slide Show** with the **Show and return** box checked. Link to it from, say, your second slide. Now practice giving a "presentation" with a jump from the second slide to the "sub-show."

Next Steps/Action Items

- See the facing page. Try this stuff when you're not under pressure to prepare a presentation. Have *fun* with it.

- Begin working these techniques into your next presentation. Don't try to do everything at once, but rather apply whatever seems to fit – and feels comfortable.

Important and most serious designs.
William Shakespeare, *Love's Labour's Lost*

Smooth success
be STREWED
before your
FEET.

PRESENTER MODE.

DAY-OF-PRESENTATION SECRETS, TIPS, TOOLS, AND TECHNIQUES.

You've created a good presentation, more compact and direct, far less wordy than anything you've done in the past.

How do you present it to maximize the impact?

Setting Up Presenter View

Presenter View shows *you* information – on your presenting computer – that's different from what the audience sees.

Presenter View makes sense only when you can see your laptop or computer monitor. If you're using a desktop computer – e.g., one hidden in a rostrum – **Presenter View** will work only if the computer allows dual displays. (Some computers are set up only to duplicate on the rostrum monitor that which is shown on the projection screen – which is another reason I use my own laptop whenever possible.)

Setting Up

At the right of the **Slide Show** menu is an area labeled **Monitors**. Make sure you've checked the **Use Presenter View** box. Normally you can leave the Monitor set to Automatic.

When you arrive at the venue to set up, assuming you have time and opportunity to do so, test the slide show to confirm that your display shows **Presenter View** rather than the projected slides. If it doesn't, exit the slide show (**Escape**) and check the **Monitor** box. Try manually setting it to the external monitor. You can also hold down the **Windows** key, press **P,** and then click **Extend**. (If neither **Extend** nor an alternate **Monitor** setting is available, the display isn't set up to support the separate **Presenter View**.)

Note that you can rearrange the windows in **Presenter View** and change the size of your notes text. Find yourself as much room for notes as possible, and make them *big enough to read at a distance*.

Plus: Practice your presentation at least once without using **Presenter View**... just in case.

Unfortunately, PowerPoint does not retain these settings between presentations, so you have to reset them every time you present. It's frustrating, but it takes only twenty seconds or so to move the windows and change text size. Make that setup a part of your pre-presentation ritual.

Using Presenter View While Speaking

The two most obvious features of **Presenter View** are a peek at the next slide, so you know what's coming, and your speaker's notes. Try not to get glued to your laptop screen or read your notes, but do what you need to be comfortable. Even in a presentation you know well, you can enhance your credibility by once or twice saying, "Let me make sure I get this exactly right," and then reading a quotation, a critical statistic, etc. from your notes.

Presenter View offers five icons in current versions of PowerPoint, as shown at right: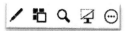

- The first gives you access to a pen, "laser pointer," and highlighter. The highlighter is useful with a touchscreen for, say, circling key points (the pen is too small to be seen easily).
- The See all slides icon, described on p. 162.
- The magnifying glass lets you enlarge part of the slide on the fly. If you're stuck with fine-print data in, say, a business review with strict formatting requirements, zoom in on the data you're talking about. Click it and move the window to highlight the part of the slide you want to enlarge. You can also "drag" the zoomed window around to enlarge different parts of the slide.
- The fourth icon blacks (and unblacks) the screen. The **B** key is easier.
- The last icon lets you jump to a Custom Show (p. 163), but it doesn't return automatically once that show ends.

Increase our wonder and set up your fame forever.
William Shakespeare, *Pericles*

Conferences: Lectern, Table, or...

You're the Only Presenter at the Session

Ditch the lectern if no one is sharing the stage for that particular session. If they can't take the lectern off the stage, push it off to the side if it's not already there (or have someone do it for you). Set yourself free.

Yes, standing with nothing between you and the audience can be scary the first time. You'll quickly get over that fear – and discover a wonderful freedom in simply talking with the audience. You can put your computer on the lectern (facing sideways) so you can see your notes in **Presenter View**, but don't anchor yourself to it.

Many conference setups have a lectern on one side of a raised stage and a set of tables that occupy the remaining stage width. Do not go behind those tables! Stand in front of them.

Presenting on a Panel

Panel discussions can be excruciatingly dull, three droning speakers accompanied by bullet-point-laden slides.

Don't fall into that trap.

Your slides don't have to be dull. They don't have to be boring. They don't have to cause dissonance between hearing and reading. Be the star of your panel, the presenter whose material strikes a chord, resonates with the audience, convinces them.

Plus: Even at the most sober professional conferences, *you* are the focus during live sessions, not your slides.

Nor do you have to sit just because you're on a panel. Stand up to make a key point. Lean over the table, staring at the audience. Even get up from the table during your section and walk around, to the front of the table or onto the floor or even among the attendees.

Sure, there are occasional staid conferences where moving around is gauche. But if you have the opportunity, take it.

Remember, your job is to make a difference to the audience… which means both you and your material must be memorable… which means you must connect.

Mobility

Take any opportunities to move down off the stage, assuming you're comfortable navigating the steps. Spending at least a little time at the audience's level helps build your connection with them. If you have an opportunity to ask them some questions, do it from floor level (at least in venues of under a few hundred people – larger, and folks in the back will have trouble seeing you).

Even if you don't have a real question opportunity, you can always do some level-setting from an equal floor level: "How many of you are attorneys?" (Or, "Who's from New Jersey?" That line isn't limited to rock concerts. Or maybe it's just that I'm writing this spread on a flight home from the Garden State.)

I walk around freely when I speak, at least at venues with less than, say, five hundred seats. If someone asks a question, for example, I want to go right up to them to offer a direct, personal answer – though of course everyone else is hearing it as well, because either I am speaking loudly or have a microphone.

Bid them cover the table.
William Shakespeare, *The Merchant of Venice*

"Audience Participation"

Experienced lawyers who argue before the U.S. Supreme Court have told me on many occasions that their #1 job at argument is to get the justices to ask questions. "The moment a justice starts talking, you stop – no matter what brilliant point of law you think you're making," as one attorney put it. They've read your briefs, have likely come to a preliminary conclusion. Your chance to sway them comes not from your words but from *theirs* – to get them discussing the case with each other!

Look for Opportunities

To a certain extent, the same holds true for presentations. For some sessions your audience has even "read the brief" – scientific papers, business reviews, etc. If your written material didn't win them over, then your presentation content may not either.

But here they are, in front of you.

By talking with them, and by getting them talking with each other, you have a one-time opportunity to sway their thinking.

Plus: Brief group exercises, if your subject and format permit, are a great way to get an audience engaged.

to Engage the Audience Directly.

Sure, it's scary.

What if they don't respond? (It happens. Be prepared to forge ahead without them. And be aware that it's often an external factor that keeps them quiet – a manager they fear, for example.)

What if you "lose control" of the session? (You won't – you're at the front of the room. And if all else fails, grab a marker and start writing something – anything! – on a white board. Conversation will die down as all eyes follow you, wanting to know what you're up to.)

One quick fix for your slides is to find or create a slide that drives the audience to participate, to speak up, to ask questions, to take a stand. That might prove to be your most effective slide!

With the participation of society.
William Shakespeare, *Henry IV pt. 2*

Presentation Timing

In the upper left hand corner of **Presenter View** sits a timer.

The timer starts the instant you launch your presentation. It doesn't know how early you set it up, allowing the audience to see your title slide as they filter it. It doesn't know how much time the host spent introducing you. And of course it doesn't know how long your presentation is supposed to be.

On the other hand, next to the timer are a **Pause/Resume** button and a **Restart** button. You'll have a leg up if you use one of them (**Restart** is easier) when you begin speaking. However, it's rather clumsy to manipulate your mouse to click a tiny icon just as you begin to speak. Thus this feature works better with touchscreens.

Above and to the right of your current slide in **Presenter View** is a time-of-day clock – like the timer, too small to read easily, but at least it's there, and it beats looking at your watch or squinting at a clock in the back of the room (if there is one).

The clock is valuable, of course, only if you know the scheduled end time for your presentation.

So figure that out before you start. Write it down on an index card or a sticky note. And remember to leave time for questions, especially if you defer them to the end of your presentation.

Timings for Half-Day or Longer Events

For a presentation that includes breaks, it's a good idea to add the target break timings to your sticky note. It's easy to get engrossed in your talk and carry on well past the break, with the audience becoming increasingly uncomfortable.

Plus: You make more friends letting the audience out five minutes early than five minutes late.

How Long Does Your Presentation Take?

When you practice your presentation, make a note of the timing, so you can get an idea of how long it will last.

This preliminary timing not only excludes questions and group exercises, but it doesn't take into account any changes in pace that you might exhibit during your presentation – e.g., speeding up from nervousness, or slowing down because you're truly observing the audience to make sure you're connecting. It also omits any on-the-fly variations – spending more time addressing one slide because you see some blank looks in the audience, glossing over another because you recognize the audience already knows or isn't interested in that material.

Still, it gives you a starting point. Over time, you'll learn how much time on average to allot for questions.

Timing Audience-Driven Sections

It's easier to time question sections than exercises. You can usually curtail or encourage questions to manipulate the total time, but it's more difficult to control exercises. Of course, you can say, "Let's spend six minutes," and cut the exercise off at that point. But some groups take longer than others to get rolling on exercises, and often you sense that they've gotten into small-group discussions at least as valuable as anything you could add.

Thus you're likely to have rough timings and/or target times on all but the shortest exercises, but actual times may vary organically. You can choose to finish early. You can cut or expand the time spent in questions. You can go into more or less detail on some slides – and it's useful to have a few of those near the end. Most of all, you can branch into optional content if time allows (p. 163), or smoothly skip slides to squeeze the time (p. 162).

The clock upbraids me with the waste of time.
William Shakespeare, *Twelfth Night*

Five Takeaways

1. **Presenter View** offers tools that help you control the presentation experience for yourself and the audience.

2. Among those tools are ways to enlarge your speaker notes to make them readable – and a timer and clock to keep you on track.

3. Get out from behind tables, lecterns, and anything else that gets between you and the audience. The goal of good slides is to help the audience focus on the important stuff – which comes from what you're saying. Don't undercut that by leaving an artificial barrier in place.

4. If you're part of a panel, set a goal of having the simplest, clearest, and most engaging slides. (That's rarely a high bar, sad to say. Half the time, you'll win that "battle" simply by ensuring your text is legible from the back of the room.)

5. Encourage questions and audience discussion. They'll learn based on what they hear from you – but they'll cement their learning from questions and discussion.

Next Steps/Action Items

- First: Get out there and fix your deck for your next presentation. Try some of these ideas – not necessarily all at once, which is overwhelming, but pick a few and implement them. Simplify your slides, using One Idea per Slide. Make sure each has a purpose. Get to know PowerPoint a little better – not necessarily to become a power user, but so that it becomes a comfortable tool rather than an awkward intermediary.

- Second: Read the next chapter, which goes beyond the quick-fix goals of the book so far and suggests a straightforward, simple way to transform not just your slides but your presentation itself.

Smooth success be strewed before your feet.
William Shakespeare, *Antony and Cleopatra*

Let us from POINT to POINT this STORY know.

TAKING IT FURTHER.

THE FIVE STEPS.

Let's close the book with an introduction to PowerPoint Plus, the Five Steps for ending Death by PowerPoint.

This book is about quick fixes, about creating slides that work, slides that support you rather than get in the way of your message. These fixes, based on the concept of One Idea per Slide, can take you a significant part of the way to an effective presentation. But they focus only on the form of one part of your presentation, the slide deck.

These final spreads offer a start in helping you shape up the other part, the content.

First, define the spine. Settle on your story, and tell it. Design, refine, maybe refine again. Practice and polish, polish and practice. Finally, deliver — and debrief afterwards.

Here's to your increasing success.

1. Define the Spine

"Spine" in this context comes from the theater, a synonym for throughline, the main thrust of a stage play (or movie).

The spine can be simple or complex, physical or psychological. *The Martian* and *E.T.* and *The Wizard of Oz*: Surviving until you can find a way home. *Macbeth*: The corrupting effects of the drive for power. *When Harry Met Sally...*: The complexity of sexually charged friendships.

Back to *Macbeth* for a minute. A director could also approach the play by saying it's about what happens when a good man allows others – his wife, the weird sisters – to override his moral compass. Or it's a Greek tragedy, wherein Macbeth finally recognizes his tragic flaw too late to change the outcome demanded by the universe. In other words, different directors can stretch the same material over different spines.

Just as you can with *your* material.

Think of the spine as your strategy, your overarching vision that proves inarguably the value of what you're presenting.

Choose One

A *Macbeth* that attempts to mix all three of my potential spines will be a muddled production - although a brilliant actor can make it hard for the audience to know what, if anything, is wrong.

So it is with presentations. A brilliant presenter can enthrall an audience despite a muddied structure, just as some actors could entertain for an hour while reading the phone book. But few of us are that brilliant. We need a spine supporting our efforts.

Plus: A spine is a strategy for "winning" – winning the audience to your point of view.

Even the most information-only presentations, such as college classes/lectures, benefit from a spine.

Did you hate history classes? Most of us did, because we got forty-five minutes of semi-random facts a few times a week. Simply connecting these facts on a timeline, the traditional history-class approach, doesn't make them feel significantly less random. If you're an American, picture a revolutionary war battle. What came to mind? The winter of Valley Forge? Wasn't even a battle! Washington crossing the Delaware? Not a battle, either, though he and his men would go on to a minor victory in Trenton the next morning. But they stick in our minds because we know stories about them, not just facts – despite the drawback that few historians would call either of these one of the ten most important battles of the American revolution.

If your goal is to inform the audience (p. 39), they will best remember what you have to say if you supply a framework – in other words, the spine. Likewise, if you want to move your audience, to affect their thinking about an issue (p. 38), you must take them on a journey of sorts from where they are to where you want them to be, also a spine (albeit of a slightly different type).

Sometimes, you're told to present topic X to group Y with viewpoint or call-to-action Z. However, in most cases, *you'll* determine the spine of your presentation.

The spine may or may not be stated outright in the slides. Consider some of the examples in the next spread:

- Compliance training, cross-group cooperation: I might use the spine as my title.
- History lecture: I might describe the examples, and then challenge the class to derive the lesson (the spine).
- IT and department funding: No outright mention of the spine, but it would inform the way I talk about every slide, even every number (at least the rolled up/total numbers).

It was the subject of my theme.
William Shakespeare, *A comedy of Errors*

Examples of Spines

Here are some ideas to stimulate your thinking. My sample spines are of course not the only way to approach these topics. My *"not"* counterexamples are all from life, and all too common. Even if you take nothing else away from this book, look at the restatements in italics – and avoid them!

Informing the Audience

Conference Session (Bad Example #2, p. 32): You can find the real meaning of Shakespeare's work by clarifying what he actually wrote. *Not: I want to share some errors in the* Macbeth *text.*

Executive Project Review: How this project is helping the company or customers. *Not: Facts and figures.* Of course you need to discuss budget and deadlines, but provide context first.

Compliance Training: Keep the company out of trouble. Or, Keep yourself out of jail. Or even, Five people who did stupid compliance tricks and got busted. *Not: Rules for compliance.*

Class Lecture: History pivots on seemingly insignificant events, as illustrated at the second day at Gettysburg. *Not: I'm supposed to teach you about Civil War history.*

Interviewing Candidates: Hiring a great team without breaking the law. Or, Why you win when you hire someone better than yourself. *Not: The techniques and laws of interviewing.*

Presenting Your Approved Budget to Your Team: Here's how we're going to do great things this year that will win customers and get you promoted. *Not. Here are our numbers. Yeah, we got cut again.*

Plus: Think about what would motivate you were you to attend one of these presentations.

Moving the Audience

Funding an IT Project (Bad Example #1, p. 30): Our company is falling behind because we're missing the kinds of breakthrough candidates that Google and Apple are recruiting. *Not: HR wants this new software system.*

Requesting Next Year's Departmental Budget: Here's the minimum it takes to do the great things next year that will win customers. *Not: Here are our numbers. Please don't cut us again.*

Sales Call: Our product makes your employees so much more productive that it will pay for itself in six months. *Not: Our product has the best/most features.*

Internal Plea for Cross-Group Cooperation: How our interests align. Or, How it benefits your career. (It depends on the organization culture.) *Not: Eat your broccoli (it's good for you), or Our CEO wants us to do this.*

After-Action Review/Project Debrief: What went well, what went not so well, and how to do more of the former and less of the latter next time. *Not: It wasn't my fault we failed.*

Make a Decision From These Alternatives: We will leave this room with a decision. *Not: Here are three options.* See p. 130.

Presentation to City Council: First, who's the audience? Officials? The public? For the former: Our supporters vote, and this matters to them. For the latter: How this will make our town a better place to live/raise children. *Not: This is incredible (or disastrous).*

Wordsmithing

Don't wordsmith the spine, agonizing over the language. It's for *you*. Sweat the words only if they wind up on a slide directly.

Oh, my son, what theme?
William Shakespeare, *Hamlet*

2. Tell Your Story

Your next step is to create a "storyboard," a movie term for a series of sketches showing how each scene is to be shot, in effect an outline (with drawings rather than words). Since PowerPoint is a visual tool, and since a good presentation tells a story, I prefer the word "storyboard" to "outline."

That said, PowerPoint has a serviceable **Outline View** that can function as a useful storyboarding tool. For all but the simplest presentations such as Bad Example #1, I recommend you approach the storyboard in two passes. First, define and locate the core elements of your story – in effect, the chapters in your book. Then, for each chapter, fill in the specific points you need to make.

Stroryboard and Story

The "story" represents a journey of sorts on which you want to take your audience.

I don't want to sound all mystical about this. It's not fiction, and I'm not going to drag in Joseph Campbell and The Hero's Journey. Nonetheless, part of your job as a presenter is to keep the audience's interest. Most people are drawn into a presentation not by a collection of facts as much as by how those facts – and theories, suggestions, visual images, questions, etc. – are assembled into a narrative by the presenter.

You are the narrator, spinning a tale with the help of visual aids (slides). You need to make that tale interesting – to the audience. (Obviously, if you're bored by it, they will be as well. Your own interest is necessary but not sufficient.)

Plus: The storyboard helps you take control of the way your presentation will convince your audience.

Story vs. Outline

What's the difference between a story and an outline?

An outline lists each key point in a proposed document, in a logical order. A story focuses on how the key points relate to the spine, and may omit various elements (slides) that would otherwise be part of an outline. Most of all, "story" reminds you of your aim: keep the audience focused on your message or convince them to alter the way they think about your topic for moving presentations.

A Storyboard Example

At right is the outline of Bad Example #1 (p. 30), the IT budget request. When I put that misbegotten deck together, I began with this outline – facts, but no spine.

1. ☐ IT Budget Meeting
2. Project Reindeer Agenda
3. Project Description
4. Why we need this project
5. Costs
6. Cost Spreadsheet
7. Timeline
8. Summary

Now consider the revised outline (with the spine as a temporary second item, italicized it so I can find it quickly). Slides 3 and 4 state the premise of the spine – we're falling behind companies like Google. Our fictional company isn't competing with Google in technology, but they *are* competing for top talent. I added a sub-item to slide 3 to remind me of the point I need to make in this regard. In this example, I haven't begun a new presentation but have built upon the existing deck. I haven't even changed the title yet. I've included the old slides at the bottom because I'll draw on that information later, especially the cost and scheduling data.

1. IT Budget Meeting
2. *We're falling behind because we're missing breakthrough candidates*
3. Falling Behind
4. We Are Competing With Google
   ▶ For talent
5. Why We Can't Find These Candidates?
6. Proposed Solution
7. Return on Investment
8. Ensuring Project Success
9. Old Slides:

I long to hear the story.
William Shakespeare, *The Tempest*

Stories From the Sample Spines

Refer to the sample spines on p. 190 as we create one possible story for many of them. I include an overly summarized spine in italics as a reminder with each one below.

Informing the Audience

Conference Session (Bad Example #2, p. 32), *clarifying Shakespeare:* Hard enough to understand. Why accept textual errors? Goal is to ensure plays flow the way they did in Willy's time. Some examples from *Macbeth*.

Executive Project Review, *helping customers:* Describe customer and business needs, the gaps between current and desired state. Project the fills gaps. Gain commitment to value before hitting budget, deadlines, project plan.

Compliance Training, *stupid compliance tricks:* Five (ex) employees who did something stupid (expect nervous laughter). Discuss the lessons and why compliance is hard, especially in the gray areas. Get audience to commit to improving, then details.

Class Lecture, *day 2, Gettysburg:* Describe all the things that went wrong for the South and ask class to derive a lesson from them, followed by more examples of history pivoting on minor incidents.

Interviewing Candidates, *hire better than yourself:* The best hires can bring new things to the table rather than replicate what we already do. It's scary to hire someone better than yourself. Explore how that actually frees you up. Close with laws and regulations.

> **Plus:** The spine leads easily to the story, which you can then expand into storyboards.

Presenting Your Approved Budget to Your Team, *goals for year:*
The company is entrusting us with money to make things happen.
Focus on results that matter. How doing great work (rather than
not-failing) leads to employee promotions.

Moving the Audience

Funding an IT Project (Bad Example #1, p. 30): *missing out on
great candidates:* See the outline/storyboard in the preceding spread.

Requesting Next Year's Departmental Budget, *helping win
customers:* Four things we can do that will matter for customers and
pay off for the business. What it costs to do them.

Sales Call, *boosting your productivity:* How our product makes your
employees so much more productive that it will pay for itself in
six months. Why it's easy to learn and easy to use.

Internal Plea for Cross-Group Cooperation, *aligning interests:* We
can both be successful if we're focused on customers, by
leveraging each other's efforts and keeping eye on big picture. Not
a zero-sum game, but an 80%/80% win/win opportunity.

After-Action Review/Project Debrief: What went well, what
went not so well, and how to do more of the former and less of
the latter next time. *(Story and spine are the same here.)*

Make a Decision From These Alternatives, *choose today:* All
options meet our minimum needs ("satisficing"), so that the cost
of delay outweighs any benefit we might get from the "perfect"
choice. Here they are. Let's pick one now.

Presentation to City Council, *influencing officials:* Vision of city
after plan in place (that you can campaign on, because supporters
are high-turnout voters). Why costs are under control.

I'll hear you more, to the bottom of your story, and never interrupt you.
William Shakespeare, *Pericles*

3. Edit and Design / Refine

This step is where you apply the majority of this book.

As you lay out ("design") your presentation, Limit the slides to a single idea each, One Idea per Slide. Remember that sometimes you'll use multiple slides to clearly express or explore that idea, but don't muddle two ideas onto a single slide.

Then for each idea/slide, determine the purpose:

- Define the Concept, introducing or explaining a concept to the audience.
- Enhance the Concept, delivering additional content that drives home you message (with no more than One Idea per Slide).
- Show Data, e.g., discus a budget, review an experiment, rank alternatives.
- Signpost, helping the audience get their bearings within a presentation (an agenda, say) or a complex idea.
- Echo the Speaker – very sporadically and carefully - to emphasize a point, spell out a definition, etc.

It's an iterative process, to the extent time permits. Each day you work on your presentation, clarify more, simplify further, explicate where necessary, and practice – not just your slides, but your words, your message, your ideas.

Start With Slide Ideas, or Your Words?

It doesn't matter.

Plus: Retain your original storyboard so you can circle back to see if you're changing your story by accident.

Some people are more comfortable focusing on how they'll say what they want to say, and then editing the slides to support them. Others use the process of working on a slide to allow their ideas about delivery of the content to germinate. It's like asking a musician whether she starts with the words or the music. Most of the time, music and lyrics move forward hand in hand. The same holds true for presentations. Whether an image or "here's what I'm going to say" takes the lead for a given idea, over time the presenter will refine both the slide and the content it supports.

Visual Design – Colors, Themes, Etc.

Don't get caught up too early in the visual design of your slides. Get your ideas "on paper" first, sketching them in rough form in PowerPoint, perhaps continuing to work in **Outline View**.

Someone whose visual style, at least for the current presentation, is image-based will probably want to begin choosing themes, colors, backgrounds, and such earlier than a text-based presenter. Working with images is easier if you know early on the type of background you'll be placing them against. Consider the light-or-dark question (p. 110) as well at this time. I recommend putting off specific formatting until the next stage – including finding a presentation style for your lists (pp. 88 and 150) and adding signposts such as agendas.

How Much Iteration?

How much time you spend on design-and-refine, how many passes you make through the material, depends on your own proclivities, the length and complexity of the content, what's at stake, and so on. Unless presenting is your main job, you're shoehorning preparation into all the other tasks that constitute your "day job." When you hit diminishing returns, move on.

You touched the life of our design.
William Shakespeare, *Troilus and Cressida*

4. Practice and Polish

As the day of your presentation approaches, spend time practicing the presentation and polishing it.

Practicing

As you develop a sequence of slides around a concept within your presentation, practice delivering it – if possible, aloud in a private setting.

As you practice, not only will you get more comfortable, but you'll discover what works and what doesn't, such as:

- I'm using lots of words to explain this. Could I do it better with a diagram? An image? A metaphor?
- Whenever I get done with this slide, I'm not sure what's next. Could the next slide be out of sequence logically or emotionally (in storytelling terms)? Do I need a transition slide?
- I keep leaving out a point I want to make. Would adding a slide remind me? Or is it not important enough to break the flow I'm developing?

If you're going to speak standing up, practice standing up. If you can't, close your eyes and visualize yourself standing as you deliver your content.

I often work on presentations on flights – and practice the sequences I'm working on by subvocalizing. (I sometimes put my head in my hands so no one sees my lips moving.) Don't try to memorize your presentation; you'll sound stilted, forced, insincere. But practice enough so that you know what you're going to say around each slide, and you know what comes next.

Plus: Just because you're polishing doesn't mean you can't go back and rework the story if you find holes.

Polishing: Bullet Lists, Images, Etc.

Now is the time to format your bullet lists (pp. 88, 150). How do they flow within your presentation? What's the right style for each list, and for your lists as a whole?

Likewise, see if your images and graphics need cleanup. Are they straight? Is the contrast good enough so that people can make sense of them in brightly lit rooms? Do you feel good about them?

Presentation Signposts

Add any necessary signposts to the presentation, such as agendas and section headings. Keep them simple – one or two words, not a treatise.

The Second Slide

The Second Slide (p. 142) drives audience involvement and engagement in your subject. What is your second slide? Is it a physical slide, or a verbal concept you'll deliver over the title slide or a blacked screen?

Although you've likely been thinking about this slide since beginning the storyboard, now is the time to be sure it feels right, looks right, and delivers the message you require of it.

Of course, this is the time to firm up your *first* slide as well, the title slide.

Professional Cleanup

If you have access to a professional cleanup service (p. 160), schedule them early – but engage them now.

I overheard him and his practices.
William Shakespeare, *As You Like It*

5. Deliver and Debrief

It's almost time to present. You've set up and practiced with **Presenter View** and multiple monitors – and at least once without **Presenter View** and onscreen access to your notes. Your slides are ready. Your clicker has fresh batteries. You have access to multiple backups of your slides (p. 170). You've worried enough for three normal people.

(Stop worrying. You'll be fine – better than fine, and way above expectations.)

Get to the venue early. Test your laptop with the projector. Walk around the room with your clicker. Adjust the size of your speaker notes in **Presenter View** (p. 176).

Use the rest room.

And relax.

Remember, the audience is there to hear *you* and wants you to succeed – whether it's an all-day training session, a conference session (panel or solo), a brief section of a business meeting, a sales presentation, or any other reason to get in front of a room, command attention, and inform and/or move the audience.

After the Presentation

Take time as soon as possible after the presentation to make some notes, perhaps in this format:

- Three things that went well.
- Three things you want to do better next time.
- Up to three bits of feedback you'd like to get.

Plus: We get better faster by asking for feedback – and then evaluating it honestly, changing as needed.

Ideally, you want to debrief with someone who attended the presentation – a colleague, the event organizer, your boss, even an attendee you run into at dinner that night. Ask them for specific feedback – what worked, what didn't, what else they'd like to see from you. (Asking for feedback is probably scarier than actually presenting… but it's the fastest way to get better.)

Don't just request generic feedback, but consider variants of the three questions noted in the preceding paragraph.

If the presentation was videotaped, watch the video in the next few days. Seeing yourself on video can be quite painful for many people, but it's a great way to isolate habits that work against you. (I know I talk too fast, ex-New-Yorker that I am. I'm working on it. Still.) It's one thing when someone tells you. It's another to see for yourself.

Feedback Forms

The ratings on feedback forms at conferences have limited utility unless you can compare your own ratings with those of other sessions you attended. Is a score of 3.6 on a scale of 1-5 good, bad, or mediocre? You don't know unless you understand how it stacks up against other presenters with similar levels of experience. (If you're a novice, don't compare yourself to a paid keynoter.) Also, the extent to which people were interested in your subject will affect your scores. I can imagine even Patrick Stewart struggling to deliver the talk behind Bad Example #2 (textual issues with *Macbeth*, p. 32) to an audience more interested in *Star Trek* than Shakespeare.

If you do get a look at feedback forms, the written-out comments can prove invaluable. Details matter far more than numbers. (And if someone hates what you did, don't take it personally. There's always someone who gets off on nasty.)

Deliver with more openness.
William Shakespeare, *Cymbeline*

~~Five~~ Six ∧Takeaways

1. **Define the spine** of your presentation, the central idea that you intend to communicate to the audience. Are you looking to move them, alter their thinking, or are you imparting information? (Or both?)

2. **Tell the story** that delivers your message. Create "storyboards" (a/k/a an outline) of your key messages in such a way that it flows, that it takes the audience on a clear journey. Consider the standard science-paper methodology: abstract, introduction, methods, results, and discussion is at heart the story of a science experiment.

3. **Define and refine** your slides and the messages (your speaking text) that will accompany each of them. Edit. Ruthlessly. Then edit (eliminate) more.

4. **Practice and polish** your presentation, both the messages you deliver verbally and the slides that support them.

5. **Deliver and debrief**. You're not done when you say, "Thank you" to the audience, unless you never give another presentation. Otherwise, perform a debrief, alone or with help. That's the fastest way to improve.

6. You do not need to do these steps in strict order, though I do think it helps to hew close to the sequence the first few times you try this method. For one thing, it'll be easier to follow along with the book, coordinating it with the work you're doing. For another, you won't get caught up in old habits, won't be nearly as tempted to "word out" the slides.

Next Steps/Action Items

- Put this book down. Get a presentation you're going to deliver, or one you want to practice with. Start trying the suggestions in this book. Figure out which ones make the most sense to you right now, and implement them. (Some of the ones that don't feel right today will make more sense in the future – and you may find some that you're never comfortable with. That's okay. Take what works for you, and run with it.)

- Remember the book next time you attend a Death by PowerPoint presentation. (It's not so you can recommend it, although such recommendations are gratefully appreciated. Rather, it will give you insight into why the presentation failed – and offer you guidance on how to keep from falling into the same traps.)

- You can explore the Back Matter to find a list of books for further reading, see what the Shakespeare quotations at the end of every spread have to do with anything, and listen to the hidden track. (The what? You'll have to browse the Back Matter to find out.)

Let us from point to point this story know.
William Shakespeare, *All's Well That Ends Well*

BACK MATTER

The back matter, sometimes called the appendix (or appendixes or appendices), is that catch-all place in a book for notes of various sorts. As the running head at the top of the page suggests, it's a bunch of other stuff.

Now I will UNCLASP a secret BOOK.

Why the Shakespeare?

What are all those Shakespeare quotes doing at the bottoms of most right-hand pages? What, I hear you asking, does Shakespeare have to do with presentations?

There's little historical evidence Willie used PowerPoint. None, actually. (Can you imagine a bullet-point version of Hamlet? No, please, please don't create one.)

But citing Shakespeare has become a tradition in each of my business books, this being the fifth in that line. I try to find new quotes each time, but there have been some repeats.

Shakespeare, of course, was a brilliant presenter, telling wonderful stories and accompanying them with living slides – a/k/a the actors. Did he think of them the way we think of slides? Probably not, especially since he was an actor himself... but on the other hand, his rules for actors, as described by Hamlet, are rather strict.

Or maybe I just like Shakespeare.

I do wonder if he'd be appalled by Bad Example #2 (p. 32), or would he appreciate the speaker's attempt to get his words exactly right? Probably a bit of both, but I suspect he'd be most frustrated at how downright boring a bad speaker could make this problem appear. Boredom in theater is a cardinal sin, and few have ever been better at avoiding it than Willie the Shake (even if not all modern actors and directors are equal to the wonderful text he gives them to explore).

Consider the "ring the bell" business on the last slide of Bad Example #2. Macduff cries, "Ring the alarum bell!" and yet the bell does not ring, not for five more lines.

Plus: Books alone aren't sufficient. See Will's plays.
(And try these tools, because reading isn't enough.)

Because if it did, you wouldn't be able to hear the rest of his speech. And that little bit about "murder and treason" is pretty important to the plot.

So Shakespeare smartly defers the actual ringing of the bell until Macduff finishes. (And yes, the repeated line is likely a stage direction that crept into the spoken text.)

Shakespeare knows that we need to focus on the speaker's words (and emotions and tone and gestures and interaction with the other characters). You are Macduff, up on your dais, your stage. You need the audience to listen to you, focus on you, not on the clanging bell of wordy, distracting slides.

Yeah, Willie would have hated bad PowerPoint decks.

That said, we can all become better presenters, with or without Will's help.

But why not add some fun to the process?

My "Rules"

I've taken all of the epigrams directly from the plays with no omitted words, and with no changes other than spelling out the occasional shortened syllable such as i' (in), th' (the), and so on. I admit to changing the sense of some quotations by starting them "in the middle" or ending them early. Shakespeare didn't write literally about slides and slide decks, so I've taken some liberties not with wording but with sentence structure.

I have also taken a bit of license with the punctuation, usually to emphasize a point. On the other hand, scholars are at odds about what punctuation Shakespeare intended. The published versions of Shakespeare's plays, the Quartos and First Folio, themselves punctuate almost randomly; neither spelling nor punctuation was consistent 400 years ago.

> *Do not saw the air too much with your hand.*
> William Shakespeare, *Hamlet*

Index

Suggested Reading

Atkinson, Cliff. 2011. *Beyond Bullet Points: Using Microsoft PowerPoint to Create Presentations That Inform, Motivate, and Inspire.* 3rd ed. Redmond, WA : Microsoft Press, 2011. Atkinson has an intresting approach to telling an emotional story via your deck that's well worth reading and considering.

Berkun, Scott. 2011. *Confessions of a Public Speaker.* Sebastopol, CA : O'Reilly Media, 2011. Berkun makes a living speaking to groups on a wide variety of topics, and has an acute level of self-awareness about speaking - what works, what doesn't, and how it all feels.

Duarte, Nacy. 2008. *slide:ology: The Art and Science of Creating Great Presentations.* Sebastopol, CA : O'Reilly Media, 2008. It's more of a design itself than a guide, but it is an interesting design, food for thought rather than a how-to guide.

Foer, Joshual. Feats of memory anyone can do. *YouTube.* [Online] [Cited: December 31, 2015.] https://www.youtube.com/watch?v=U6PoUg7jXsA.

Gallo, Carmine. 2015. *Talk Like TED: The 9 Public-Speaking Secrets of the World's Top Minds.* New York, NY : St. Martin's Griffin, 2015. Idiosyncratic, heavy handed about the need for passion (though the need is real enough), and missing some key elements of TED success (e.g., practice and more practice), it nevertheless offers solid insights into the best of these eighteen-minute talks.

—. 2009. *The Presentation Secrets of Steve Jobs: How to Be Insanely Great in Front of Any Audience.* New York : McGraw-Hill, 2009. It's interesting to see how hard he worked to keep it simple. His presentations were models of focus.

Helmke, Matt. Presentation Zen: An Overview. *YouTube.* [Online] [Cited: December 31, 2015.] https://www.youtube.com/watch?v=50mHX8_B5-s.

Kahneman, Daniel. 2011. *Thinking, Fast and Slow.* New York : Farrar, Straus, and Giroux, 2011. How and why we decide.

Lessig, Lawrence. "Republic, Lost" | Talks at Google. *YouTube.* [Online] [Cited: December 31, 2015.] https://www.youtube.com/watch?v=Ik1AK56FtVc.

Levy, Steven B. 2012. *The Off Switch: Discovering Your Work-Work Balance.* Seattle : DayPack Books, 2012. The casebook for managing time in today's always-on environments.

Norvig, Peter. The Gettysburg PowerPoint Presentation. *Norvig.com.* [Online] [Cited: December 31, 2015.] http://norvig.com/Gettysburg/.

Reynolds, Garr. 2011. *Presentation Zen: Simple Ideas on Presentation Design and Delivery.* 2nd ed. Berkeley, CA : New Riders, 2011. A must-read book about why slide design matters, full of elegant and inspiring examples.

—. TEDxTokyo - Garr Reynolds - Lessons from the Bamboo - [English]. *YouTube.* [Online] [Cited: December 31, 2015.] https://www.youtube.com/watch?v=9g8T8MsFIp0.

Shakespeare, William. 1623. First Folio. *Internet Shakespeare Editions.* [Online] 1623. Catch up with Willy via your local theater companies. He's got a lot to say about presentation. I worked from a reproduction of the First Folio, but you can easily find it on line. http://internetshakespeare.uvic.ca.

The Hidden Track

CDs – remember when music arrived on physical objects? – sometimes have a hidden track beyond the last one listed on the cover, so why not a "hidden track" in a book?

The hidden secret of great slides is visible on the screen at the front of the room only should the speaker happen to walk in front of the projector.

That hidden secret is, of course, you.

Even the most beautiful slides – from Garr Reynolds, say, or Nancy Duarte – are relatively insignficant to the audience, however much another presenter might admire them. Great slides support the speaker, reinforce concepts, maybe provide a metaphor or "back entrance" to drive home the speaker's meaning.

But even the most elegant slides are nothing but bric-a-brac, random decoration, without that speaker. without the presenter's words – and tone, and gestures, and presence.

Job #1: Don't Let Your Slides

You don't need spectacular slides to succeed. Far more important is to develop a deck that doesn't compete with you, one that doesn't detract from your presentation, impede your message, stealing or dividing the audience's attention precisely when you need them to attend to a critical idea.

Plus: The definition of insanity is doing the same thing and expecting different results.

Get in Your Way!

Supposedly when the Pope asked Michelangelo how he'd created his majestic sculpture of David, the artist replied, "I just carved away everything that didn't look like David."

Start carving. The more that's *not* there, the better your slides will serve you.

Now I will unclasp a secret book.
William Shakespeare, *Henry IV pt. 1*

About the Author

Steven B. Levy is a business leader, public speaker, project manager, author, and the CEO of Lexician, which provides training, coaching, and consulting on presentation, project management, and leadership.

Previously, he headed Microsoft's legal technology / operations department, led two product groups, co-headed application development in IT, and managed multi-million-dollar consulting projects in his seventeen years at the company. He specialized in innovation, leadership, customer and client focus, and team effectiveness.

His unique and practical approach to leadership, people and project management, and workplace effectiveness is based on thirty-five years of managing projects and leading businesses on three continents. His work has made him a highly requested speaker, trainer, and seminar leader.

His previous books include the groundbreaking *Legal Project Management: Control Costs, Meet Schedules, Manage Risks, and Maintain Sanity,* the thought-provoking *The Off Switch: Discovering Your Work-Work Balance,* and the introduction to the LPM field, *Legal Project Management Field Guide: Five Tools for Busy Professionals.*

He divides his time among Seattle, the San Juan Islands of Washington State, and cities around the globe helping clients.